Holt Spanish Level 2

¡Ven conmigo!®

Grammar and Vocabulary
Workbook

Teacher's Edition
with Answer Key

HOLT, RINEHART AND WINSTON
Harcourt Brace & Company

Austin • New York • Orlando • Atlanta • San Francisco • Boston • Dallas • Toronto • London

Cover Illustration Credit
Eva Vagretti Cockrille

¡VEN CONMIGO! is a registered trademark licensed to Holt, Rinehart and Winston.

Printed in the United States of America

ISBN 0-03-052709-0

1 2 3 4 5 6 7   021   03 02 01 00 99

Contents

To the Teacher

An important component of language proficiency is accuracy. The *Grammar and Vocabulary Reteaching and Practice Workbook* is designed to give students more practice in gaining accuracy with the structures, words, and phrases in each **paso** of *¡Ven conmigo!*

The number of worksheets for each chapter is determined by the amount of material in each **paso** that is suitable for additional focused practice.

In general, the activities in each chapter of the *Grammar and Vocabulary Reteaching and Practice Workbook* targets the vocabulary and grammar presented in that chapter. Following the philosophy of the *¡Ven conmigo!* series, the activities may also include grammar and vocabulary that have been recycled from earlier chapters.

Every major grammar concept from the *Pupil's Edition* is re-presented in this workbook so that students have another opportunity to understand these concepts before attempting to practice them again. The functions and functional expressions (**Así se dice**) are practiced selectively as needed.

Answers, arranged by chapter, are provided at the end of the book.

CAPÍTULO

1 Mis amigos y yo

■ PRIMER PASO

To introduce yourself and others, you'll need to use the verb **tener**. To describe people, you'll need to use adjectives and words that express nationality.

¿Te acuerdas? The verb **tener**   *Pupil's Edition, p. 9*

The verb **tener** *(to have)* is irregular in the present tense.

yo **tengo**	nosotros **tenemos**
tú **tienes**	vosotros tenéis
él / ella / usted **tiene**	ellos / ellas / ustedes **tienen**

---

1 Enrique is telling his new friend Andrés about his family. Complete his sentences with the correct form of **tener.**

1. Yo _____ un hermano y dos hermanas.

2. Ésta es mi hermana Ana. _____ 21 años.

3. Mis hermanos Carlos y Rebeca no están aquí porque _____ clase.

4. Ana tiene un carro nuevo, pero Carlos, Rebeca y yo no _____ coche.

5. Oye, Andrés, ¿cuántos hermanos _____ tú?

6. Y tus hermanos, ¿cuántos años _____?

2 You overhear parts of a conversation between Mr. Robles and his new neighbor Juanita. Complete the missing portions of their conversation.

JUANITA   ¿(1) _____, señor?

SR. ROBLES   Tengo 45 años.

JUANITA   ¿Tienen hijos usted y su esposa?

SR. ROBLES   No, (2) _____. Tienes dos hermanos, ¿no?

JUANITA   Sí, (3) _____.

SR. ROBLES   ¿(4) _____?

JUANITA   No, no tenemos amigos en Granada.

SR. ROBLES   ¿(5) _____?

JUANITA   No, no tengo carro todavía. Solo tengo 15 años.

---

*G*ramática de repaso Adjective agreement *Pupil's Edition, p. 11*

1. In general, adjectives that end in **-o** are masculine, and adjectives that end in **-a** are feminine.

   Carlos es alt**o** y Cristina es alt**a** también.

2. Adjectives that end in a consonant or with **-e** usually don't change to agree in gender.

   Verónica es jove**n**, fuert**e** y lea**l** *(loyal)*.

3 Mark's friend Linda is moving to his town. He wrote this letter to tell her what to expect in her new high school. Fill in the blanks with the correct form of the adjectives in parentheses.

Linda,

Hay algunas cosas que necesitas saber. Primero, debes estudiar mucho para la clase de la señora Lee. Su clase es muy **(1)** _____ (difícil). Atención en la clase de la señora Radke . . . no es muy **(2)** _____ (simpático). Si estás en el equipo de baloncesto, debes ser muy **(3)** _____ (atlético) porque el equipo juega por tres horas cada día. Mi profesora favorita es la señorita Hendricks. Es muy **(4)** _____ (tímido) pero es una profesora **(5)** _____ (excelente).

Tu amigo, Mark

4 How would you describe the following people? Complete each sentence with the correct forms of two adjectives from the word bank.

inteligente	leal	simpático	moreno
cariñoso	joven rubio	alegre	guapo

1. Yo soy _____ .

2. Mi actriz favorita es _____ .

3. Mi actor favorito es _____ .

4. Mi profesora favorita es _____ .

5. Mi mejor amigo es _____ .

> **G**ramática de repaso   Adjectives of nationality,   *Pupil's Edition, p. 11*
> -**dor** adjectives
>
> 3. Adjectives ending in -**dor** and adjectives of nationality end in -**a** in the feminine.
>
>   Marta es española. Es muy trabajadora *(hard-working)*.

5 How would you describe these people? Based on the clues given, write a description for each person, using the correct forms of the appropriate adjectives from the word bank.

MODELO   Luisa no trabaja mucho.   **Luisa no es muy trabajadora.**

español	colombiano	mexicano	hablador	italiano

1. Carlos es de México. _____ .

2. Marie-Claire no habla mucho. _____ .

3. Andrea es de España. _____ .

4. Giovanni es de Italia. _____ .

5. Graciela no es de Colombia. _____ .

> **G**ramática de repaso   Plural of adjectives   *Pupil's Edition, p. 11*
>
> 4. To make an adjective plural, add -**s** if the adjective ends in a vowel or -**es** if it ends in a consonant.
>
>   Enrique y Susana son jóven**es** y muy simpático**s**.

6 Paola is describing people she met at summer band camp. Complete her descriptions with the correct forms of appropriate adjectives from the word bank.

fuerte	calvo	artístico	viejo	
	hablador	extrovertido		francés

1. Meg y Julie son ingleses. Pero Gus y Karl no son ingleses; son _____ .

2. Quiero consejeros *(advisers)* jóvenes pero todos nuestros consejeros son _____ .

3. El Sr. Guzmán y el Sr. Cela no tienen mucho pelo. Son casi _____ .

4. Franco y Denisa hablan mucho. Son _____ .

5. José levanta pesas conmigo. José y yo somos muy _____ .

6. Susan y Donna tocan tres instrumentos y pintan también. Son muy _____ .

VOCABULARIO   Nationalities   *Pupil's Edition, p. 12*

7 Complete the crossword puzzle with the appropriate words of nationality.

Verticales

1. Una chica de Colombia es _____.
2. Un profesor de Guatemala es _____.
3. Una doctora de Uruguay es _____.
5. Una veterinaria de Honduras es _____.

Horizontales

4. Una mujer del Ecuador es _____.
6. Unos doctores de México son _____.
7. Una profesora de Paraguay es _____.
8. Un dentista de la República Dominicana es _____.

8 Héctor and Celia are trying to think of a famous person from every country in the Americas. Based on Celia's answers, write Héctor's questions.

MODELO   HÉCTOR   **¿Es mexicano Luis Miguel?**

CELIA   Sí, Luis Miguel es de México.

HÉCTOR   **(1)** ¿_____?

CELIA   Sí, creo que Rubén Blades es de Panamá.

HÉCTOR   **(2)** ¿_____?

CELIA   ¿Tish Hinojosa? Sí, es de los Estados Unidos.

HÉCTOR   **(3)** ¿_____?

CELIA   Sí, Iván Hernández es de Cuba. Es beisbolista, ¿no?

HÉCTOR   **(4)** ¿_____?

CELIA   La escritora Isabel Allende... sí, es de Chile, creo.

HÉCTOR   **(5)** ¿_____?

CELIA   Sí, tienes razón... Mario Vargas Llosa es de Perú.

¡Ven conmigo! Level 2, Chapter 1

■ SEGUNDO PASO

To talk about what you and others do, you'll need to use the present tense of regular verbs. You'll also need to use some irregular verbs and the **ir a** + *infinitive* construction.

*G*ramática de repaso   Present tense of regular verbs   *Pupil's Edition, p. 16*

In Spanish, the ending of each verb indicates who is doing the action, so you usually don't need to include subject pronouns.

	NADAR	COMER	ESCRIBIR
yo	nad**o**	com**o**	escrib**o**
tú	nad**as**	com**es**	escrib**es**
él / ella / usted	nad**a**	com**e**	escrib**e**
nosotros	nad**amos**	com**emos**	escrib**imos**
vosotros	nad**áis**	com**éis**	escrib**ís**
ellos / ellas / ustedes	nad**an**	com**en**	escrib**en**

9 Miguel Montesinos, a rock star, was interviewed by *Rock 21* about what he does when on tour. Complete the article with the appropriate forms of the verbs in parentheses.

Toco la guitarra y mis compañeros Aidan y Trent

(1)_____ (tocar) los otros instrumentos. Yo

(2)_____ (cantar) todas mis canciones nuevas. Después

de cada concierto mis compañeros y yo **(3)**_____

(mirar) el video del concierto y **(4)**_____ (comer)

algo. Por la noche Trent **(5)**_____ (escribir) nuevas

canciones.

10 Blanca conducted a video survey of what people do after school. Complete the videoscript with the correct forms of the most appropriate verbs from the word bank.

1. Samira _____ cartas a sus amigos.

2. Alfonsina y Adriano _____ en el lago.

3. Evangelina y yo _____ música en la radio.

4. Yo _____ un sándwich y _____ un vaso de leche.

5. Ana, tú _____ a una clase de ejercicios, ¿no?

6. Todos los estudiantes _____ la ropa los sábados.

lavar   comer
asistir   tomar
escuchar
escribir   nadar
limpiar

¿Te acuerdas? The verbs **salir, venir, hacer,** *Pupil's Edition, p. 16*
ver, and ir

Here are the forms of the irregular verbs **salir, venir, hacer, ver,** and **ir.**

SALIR	VENIR	HACER	VER	IR
salgo	**vengo**	**hago**	veo	voy
sales	**vienes**	haces	ves	**vas**
sale	**viene**	hace	ve	va
salimos	venimos	hacemos	vemos	**vamos**
salís	venís	hacéis	veis	**vais**
salen	**vienen**	hacen	ven	van

11 On the way to the school cafeteria, you overhear the following bits of conversations. Complete the conversations using the correct forms of the verbs in parentheses.

AMPARO Hola, Carlos, ¿qué **(1)** _____ (hacer) esta tarde?

CARLOS **(2)** _____ (ir) al mercado, ¿y tú?

HAROLD ¿A qué hora **(3)** _____ (salir) de tu clase de inglés?

ADRIANA **(4)** _____ (salir) a las tres.

BETH ¿A qué hora **(5)** _____ (venir) a mi casa a estudiar?

EDUARDO **(6)** _____ (venir) más tarde, a las siete y media.

VICTORIA ¿**(7)** _____ (ver) ustedes muchas películas?

BECKY Sí, **(8)** _____ (ver) una película todos los sábados.

12 Trevor is trying to find out more about a classmate, Marie. Write Marie's negative answers to Trevor's questions.

MODELO TREVOR ¿Sales del trabajo muy tarde?
          MARIE **No, no salgo del trabajo muy tarde.**

TREVOR ¿Vienes temprano *(early)* al colegio?

MARIE **(1)** _____ .

TREVOR ¿Salen mucho tú y tus amigos los fines de semana?

MARIE **(2)** _____ .

TREVOR ¿Haces tu tarea en la biblioteca?

MARIE **(3)** _____ .

TREVOR ¿Ve tu familia mucho la televisión?

MARIE **(4)** _____ .

TREVOR ¿Vas con tu hermana a la fiesta de Gisela?

MARIE **(5)** _____ .

> ## ¿Te acuerdas? ir a + *infinitive*   *Pupil's Edition, p. 17*
>
> Use **ir a** + *infinitive* to tell what someone is going to do.
>
> Maribel **va a jugar** al tenis esta tarde.   ¿**Vas a asistir** al partido?

13 Virginia is talking about what she and her friends are going to do this weekend. Complete her sentences with **ir a** + *infinitive,* according to the model.

MODELO   Nosotros vamos a jugar al béisbol pero Enrique <u>va a comer</u> (comer).

1. Antonio va a ir a la playa pero yo _____ (estudiar).

2. Flavio va a escuchar la radio pero Emiliano _____ (correr).

3. Hans y Greta van a nadar pero José y Margarita _____ (ver) una película venezolana.

4. Fermín y Naoko van a asistir a un concierto pero yo no _____ (estar) allí.

5. Ann va a bailar pero Tim y yo _____ (leer) en la biblioteca.

14 Enrique is telling you what he and his friends usually do on Friday afternoons. Using **ir a** + *infinitive,* rewrite his sentences to tell what he and his friends are going to do next Friday.

MODELO   Escucho la radio.   **Voy a escuchar la radio.**

1. Hago la tarea. _____

2. Eva y yo comemos en el Café Triomphe. _____

3. Sandra escribe en su diario *(diary).* _____

4. Eladio y Graciela escuchan la radio. _____

5. Y tú juegas al tenis. _____

15 Jamal is surveying shoppers to find out what products and services the local mall needs to provide. Based on their responses, write the questions he asked.

JAMAL   **(1)** ¿ _____?

SRA. WARREN   No, no voy a comprar un televisor este año.

JAMAL   **(2)** ¿ _____?

ANA Y JUAN   Vamos a ver tres películas este mes.

JAMAL   **(3)** ¿ _____?

ALBERTO   Sí, voy a jugar al tenis esta semana.

JAMAL   **(4)** ¿ _____?

SHAUNA   Voy a mandar un fax esta semana.

JAMAL   **(5)** ¿ _____?

SR. ARCE   No, mis hijos no van a necesitar instrumentos musicales este semestre.

■ TERCER PASO

To say what you like and don't like, you'll need to use the verb **gustar** and similar verbs with indirect object pronouns.

¿Te acuerdas? gusta and gustan *Pupil's Edition, p. 21*

- Use **gusta** when you're talking about liking one thing. For more than one thing, use **gustan.**

    A mí me **gusta** el tenis pero a Paul no le **gustan** los deportes.

- With one or more infinitives, use **gusta.**

    Me **gusta** correr y hacer ejercicios aeróbicos.

---

16 José Luis is talking about what he and his friends like and don't like at school. Complete his sentences with **gusta** or **gustan.**

1. No nos _____ la comida de la cafetería.

2. A mí me _____ la clase de inglés.

3. No le _____ a Héctor las matemáticas.

4. No les _____ a Rosaura y a Dennis las clases de literatura.

5. A Carlos le _____ tocar un instrumento en la banda.

6. ¿A ti te _____ los equipos *(teams)* de la escuela?

7. A José le _____ hablar español en su clase de español.

8. A Ana no le _____ los ejercicios aeróbicos.

17 Write a sentence in Spanish indicating whether you like or don't like the things or activities mentioned below.

1. la música rock _____

2. la comida china _____

3. leer y aprender _____

4. las legumbres _____

5. hablar con mis amigos _____

6. escuchar música clásica _____

7. asistir a mis clases _____

8. ver la televisión _____

9. correr _____

10. escribir composiciones _____

¿Te acuerdas? Indirect object pronouns with *Pupil's Edition, p. 21*
gustar and other verbs

To indicate who likes or doesn't like something, use the indirect object pronouns **me,
te, le, nos, os,** and **les** with verbs like **gustar, encantar, fascinar,** and **chocar.**

Me encanta la música de Luis Rafael. Nos fascina ir al cine.

18 Kimiko, Martina, and Mr. Nichols are talking about their likes, dislikes, and interests.
Complete their conversation with the missing indirect object pronouns.

KIMIKO A mí **(1)** _____ fascina el arte de la América Latina.

¿**(2)** _____ gusta a ti, Martina?

MARTINA A mí no **(3)** _____ gusta mucho, pero a mi amiga Severina

(4) _____ encanta ver programas sobre el arte en la televisión.

Sr. Nichols, ¿**(5)** _____ chocan a usted los programas en la televisión?

SR. NICHOLS Al contrario. A mi familia y a mí **(6)** _____ encanta la televisión.

Oigan *(listen)*, ¿**(7)** _____ gustan a ustedes las películas de

Andrés Galindo?

KIMIKO Ay, sí, a Martina y a mí **(8)** _____ encantan. A nosotras

(9) _____ gusta mucho su nueva película *Los globos rojos.*

19 Answer the following questionnaire about your family's interests. You can answer positively
or negatively. Use verbs like **encantar, fascinar,** and **chocar** in your answers.

Centro de recreo
Tel. 875-35-36

CUESTIONARIO

1. ¿Le gusta a usted visitar museos?

_____

2. ¿Les gusta a usted y a su familia pasear en bicicleta?

_____

3. ¿Les gusta a sus hermanos ir a conciertos de música rock?

_____

4. ¿Le gustan a usted los videojuegos?

_____

5. ¿Le gustan los deportes a su familia?

_____

2 Un viaje al extranjero

■ PRIMER PASO

To talk about how you're feeling, you'll need to use the verb **estar** and adjectives.

> **¿Te acuerdas?** The verb **estar** *Pupil's Edition, p. 35*
>
> Remember to use **estar** to describe changing moods and physical conditions.
>
> | | |
> |---|---|
> | yo **estoy** | nosotros **estamos** |
> | tú **estás** | vosotros estáis |
> | él / ella / usted **está** | ellos / ellas / ustedes **están** |

1 Complete this answering machine message with the correct forms of **estar**.

Hola, Vero, ¿qué tal? Habla Maribel. Voy a Chicago mañana y
(1) _____ muy contenta. Mis padres (2) _____ un poco
preocupados pero eso es normal. Ay, tengo mucho que hacer. ¿(3) _____
ocupada tú? ¿Me ayudas? Pablo no viene a ayudarme porque (4) _____
enfermo. Si nosotras no (5) _____ cansadas, podemos ir a su casa
a las ocho para visitarlo. ¡Chao!

2 Maribel is describing how she and others are feeling. Complete her description according to the model. Remember to use the correct form of the adjective.

MODELO   Juana / estar / contento
Juana está contenta.

1. Robertín / estar / muy aburrido

_____

2. Mis padres / estar / triste

_____

3. Yo / estar / nervioso

_____

4. Verónica y yo / estar / ocupado

_____

5. Mi padre / estar / enfadado

_____

3 The following people are on vacation. Based on each description, choose the best adjective and write a sentence describing how that person or group feels.

1. Antes de ir a Madrid mañana, Elena necesita comprar muchas cosas, visitar a su abuela e ir al banco.

   (aburrido, ocupado) _____

2. Rafael no está contento. Necesita regresar a Miami pero sus amigos no pueden ir con él.

   (triste, cansado) _____

3. José Luis y Alejo no tienen nada que hacer. Están de vacaciones en la playa pero está lloviendo y no pueden salir de la casa.

   (aburrido, contento) _____

4. Nosotros fuimos a los museos esta mañana y esta tarde fuimos al teatro.

   (nervioso, cansado) _____

VOCABULARIO   How people are feeling   *Pupil's Edition, p. 36*

4 Unscramble the words to create appropriate captions for the following pictures.

1.   2.   3.   4.

   izlfe   rdiimoepd   cdnoeaomio   ed lam ruomh

_____   _____   _____   _____

5 These people are waiting for their plane. Write sentences about how they're feeling, using adjectives from the word bank.

> tranquilo   emocionado   triste   aburrido
> ocupado   enfermo   cansado

1. Roberto tiene muchísimas ganas de ver a sus abuelos. Siempre está feliz con ellos.

   _____

2. Claudia está llorando porque va a Los Ángeles y su perro no puede ir con ella.

   _____

3. Mario no tiene nada que hacer. Tiene ganas de hacer algo interesante.

   _____

4. El señor Obregón nunca está preocupado cuando hace un viaje.

   _____

5. Miguel y Juana compraron una pizza, dos hamburguesas y papas fritas. También tomaron cuatro refrescos.

   _____

■ SEGUNDO PASO

To say if something has already been done, you'll need to use adverbs of time, the preterite of regular -**ar** verbs and of the verb **ir**, and vocabulary that refers to places around town. To ask for and offer help, you'll need to use the verbs **querer** and **poder**.

VOCABULARIO   Adverbs of time   *Pupil's Edition, p. 38*

6 It's 2 p.m. on Saturday, July 29, and Humberto is getting ready to leave for Puerto Rico. Look at his daily planner and match his activities with the time he did them.

CALENDARIO						
DOMINGO	**LUNES**	**MARTES**	**MIERCOLES**	**JUEVES**	**VIERNES**	**SÁBADO**
23	24 *comprar boleto* ✓	25	26	27 *ir al banco* ✓	28 *7:00 a.m. lavar ropa* ✓ *9:00 p.m. hacer maletas* ✓	29 *9:00 a.m. llamar taxi* ✓

_____ 1. Hizo las maletas.

_____ 2. Compró su boleto para Puerto Rico.

_____ 3. Llamó un taxi.

_____ 4. Fue al Banco Central.

_____ 5. Lavó la ropa.

a. ayer por la mañana

b. anteayer

c. esta mañana

d. el lunes pasado

e. anoche

7 Now describe how Humberto got ready for his trip by writing sentences combining the information in the two columns in Activity 6 and putting them in the correct order.

1. _____

_____

2. _____

_____

3. _____

_____

4. _____

_____

5. _____

Gramática de repaso   Preterite of regular -ar verbs   *Pupil's Edition, p. 39*

If you want to talk about what happened or what someone did, use the preterite tense. To form the preterite tense of **hablar** or any other regular **-ar** verb, take the stem of the verb (**habl-**) and add these endings:

yo habl**é**	nosotros habl**amos**
tú habl**aste**	vosotros hablasteis
él / ella / usted habl**ó**	ellos / ellas / ustedes habl**aron**

8 Complete Humberto's postcard with the correct forms of the verbs from the word bank.

bailar	tomar	llegar	bucear	regresar

Aquí estoy en Puerto Rico con mi familia. Nosotros
(1) _____ a la isla el sábado a las 9:00 de la noche.
El domingo por la mañana mis padres (2) _____ en
el Caribe y mi hermana y yo (3) _____ el sol.
Mi hermana (4) _____ al hotel porque estaba
cansada. Por la noche fui a una fiesta y (5) _____
con unos amigos. Bueno, hoy es lunes y las vacaciones continúan.
¡Qué felicidad!

Humberto

9 A tour guide is asking Mr. Silva what he and his family did on vacation in Guadalajara. Write his responses using the preterite tense.

MODELO   ¿Fueron a muchos restaurantes?
    Sí, fuimos a muchos restaurantes.

1. ¿Visitaron el mercado Libertad?

    Sí, _____.

2. ¿Tomó usted muchas fotos?

    No, _____.

3. ¿Mandó usted las postales *(postcards)*?

    No, _____.

4. ¿Compraron ustedes regalos para sus amigos?

    Sí, _____.

10 Write questions for the answers below, using **dónde, cuándo, cuánto, qué,** and **cómo.**

1. ¿ _____ ?

   Compré los billetes en Viajes Somos Nosotros.

2. ¿ _____ ?

   Marta y Miguel pagaron 26 dólares por la maleta.

3. ¿ _____ ?

   Nosotros hablamos con el tío Martín anteayer.

4. ¿ _____ ?

   Paula y Esteban llegaron a la casa del tío Martín en autobús.

¿Te acuerdas? The preterite of the verb **ir**   *Pupil's Edition, p. 41*

yo **fui**	nosotros **fuimos**
tú **fuiste**	vosotros fuisteis
él / ella / usted **fue**	ellos / ellas / ustedes **fueron**

---

11 Sara and Tomás are retracing their steps trying to remember where Tomás left his wallet. Complete what Tomás says with the correct preterite forms of the verb **ir.**

El sábado pasado nosotros (1) _____ a la casa de Roberto y Éster. A las

doce Sara (2) _____ al parque con Éster y yo (3) _____ al

partido de fútbol con Roberto. Después de ir al parque nosotros (4) _____ a

comer al Restaurante Cómelotodo antes de regresar a casa. Después del partido Roberto

(5) _____ al trabajo y yo regresé a casa. Ay no, yo (6) _____ al

café antes de regresar a casa; allí debe de estar.

¿Se te ha olvidado? Places around town   *Pupil's Edition, p. 336*

12 Roberto is going to New York to visit his family. Match the places he'll visit with the things that he'll see at each place, and write the matching phrases in the blanks provided.

_____	1. la biblioteca	**a.** una película cómica
_____	2. el centro comercial	**b.** muchos libros
_____	3. el cine	**c.** el arte de Botero
_____	4. el museo	**d.** unos animales exóticos
_____	5. el zoológico	**e.** el correo
		f. unas tiendas de ropa

13 Irene is talking about what everyone did last weekend. Indicate where she and her friends went according to the model.

MODELO   Yo vi unos tigres.   Yo **fui al zoológico.**

1. Félix y yo bailamos toda la noche.

   Félix y yo _____

   _____.

2. Flo y Mika mandaron unas cartas.

   Flo y Mika _____

   _____.

3. Estudié mucho.

   Yo _____

   _____.

4. Guadalupe y Fernando miraron una película.

   Guadalupe y Fernando _____

   _____.

5. Y compraste un estéreo, ¿no?

   Y tú _____

   _____.

Nota Gramatical   The present tense of **querer**   *Pupil's Edition, p. 42*
and **poder**

Querer and **poder** are irregular in the present tense.

QUERER		PODER	
quiero	queremos	puedo	podemos
quieres	queréis	puedes	podéis
quiere	quieren	puede	pueden

14 Mario is talking about things he and his friends want to do but can't. Complete the sentences with the correct forms of **querer** or **poder.**

1. Yo _____ comprar un videojuego pero no _____ porque no tengo dinero.
2. Beti y Lila _____ ir al cine pero no _____ porque no tienen tiempo.
3. Ron y yo _____ correr pero no _____ porque estamos cansados.
4. Rafi _____ bailar pero no _____ porque tiene que estudiar.
5. Juan _____ levantar pesas pero no _____ porque está enfermo.
6. Y tú _____ dormir ¡pero no _____ porque tienes que trabajar!

CAPÍTULO 2 Segundo paso

■ TERCER PASO

To describe your city or town, you might want to use the verb **estar** to say where things are located. You also might want to use weather expressions.

¿Te acuerdas? Using **estar** to indicate location   *Pupil's Edition, p. 45*

Use **estar** to tell where people or things are located.

Alfredo y Luisa **están** en el centro comercial.

---

15 Soraya works for her city's Chamber of Commerce. Using the correct forms of **estar**, complete her telephone conversation with a visitor who has called for information.

SRA. VILLA   Buenas tardes, señorita. Mi esposo y yo **(1)** _____

en su ciudad por tres días pero no sé dónde **(2)** _____

muchos lugares. ¿Me puede decir por favor dónde **(3)** _____

el correo, el Teatro Colón y el Museo de Arte?

SORAYA   Con mucho gusto, señora. ¿En qué hotel **(4)** _____ ustedes?

SRA. VILLA   Nosotros **(5)** _____ en el Hotel Marsella.

SORAYA   Ah, sí, claro. El Hotel Marsella **(6)** _____ en la Calle

Dieciséis. El correo **(7)** _____ muy cerca en la Calle

Dieciocho. Y el Teatro Colón y el Museo de Arte **(8)** _____

en la Calle Veinticuatro, cerca del Centro Comercial Miraflores.

SRA. VILLA   Gracias, señorita. Adiós.

16 How would your best friend ask you . . . ?

1. where you are

   ¿ _____ ?

2. where your parents are

   ¿ _____ ?

3. where the two of you are

   ¿ _____ ?

4. where your car is

   ¿ _____ ?

5. where his books are

   ¿ _____ ?

¡Ven conmigo! Level 2, Chapter 2

CAPÍTULO 2 Tercer paso

VOCABULARIO   Weather expressions   *Pupil's Edition, p. 46*

17 Cristina's weekend plans often depend on the weather. Write the letter of the weather expression that corresponds best to each plan.

_____ 1. Voy a esquiar con mi familia.

_____ 2. Voy a ir a la playa con mis amigos.

_____ 3. Voy a caminar con mis amigos.

_____ 4. Voy a mirar una película en casa porque no quiero salir.

a. Hace sol y calor.

b. Llueve mucho.

c. Hace fresco.

d. Hace mucho frío y nieva.

18 Look at the following weather report and tell what the weather is like in the following cities.

Madrid		69° F	Mallorca		96° F
Barcelona		52° F	Pamplona		38° F
Sevilla		75° F	La Coruña		40° F

1. En Sevilla _____

2. En La Coruña _____

3. En Mallorca _____

4. En Madrid _____

5. En Barcelona _____

6. En Pamplona _____

¿Se te ha olvidado?   Clothing   *Pupil's Edition, p. 336*

19 Answer the following questions using appropriate weather and clothing expressions.

1. ¿Qué tiempo hace en tu ciudad en el verano? ¿Qué ropa te pones?

_____

2. ¿Cuándo nieva en tu ciudad? ¿Qué ropa te pones?

_____

3. ¿Qué tiempo hace en marzo y en abril? ¿Qué vas a llevar?

_____

4. ¿Qué tiempo hace en septiembre y en octubre? ¿Y qué vas a llevar?

_____

CAPÍTULO 2 Tercer paso

CAPÍTULO 3

La vida cotidiana

■ PRIMER PASO

To talk about your daily routine, you'll need to use the appropriate vocabulary, reflexive verbs and pronouns, the verb **vestirse,** and adverbs.

VOCABULARIO   Daily routine   *Pupil's Edition, p. 63*

1 Write the word in each list that doesn't belong.

1. la ropa, ponerse, quitarse, vestirse, el peine   _____

2. el pelo, levantarse, el cepillo, el champú, el peine   _____

3. el jabón, despertarse, el despertador, levantarse, acostarse   _____

4. el jabón, la toalla, vestirse, bañarse, el champú   _____

2 Diana is explaining her daily routine to her little sister. Complete her explanation using items from the word bank.

| el peine   el champú   el espejo   la pasta de dientes |
| me miro   el despertador   la secadora de pelo |

1. Me despierto cada mañana cuando suena *(rings)* _____.

2. Me baño y me lavo el pelo con _____.

3. Luego me seco el pelo con _____.

4. Me lavo los dientes después con _____.

5. Luego _____ en el espejo.

¿Te acuerdas?   Personal grooming   *Pupil's Edition, p. 63*

3 Mrs. Pastor is reviewing good health and grooming habits with her class. Choose the verb that best completes each sentence and write it in the blank provided.

1. Usan el jabón para _____.

2. Deben usar el peine para _____.

3. Necesitan usar la pasta de dientes para _____.

4. Las muchachas van a usar un espejo para _____.

5. Y en dos o tres años, los muchachos van a _____.

| afeitarse |
| maquillarse |
| ducharse |
| lavarse los |
| dientes |
| acostarse |
| peinarse |

*G*ramática Reflexive verbs and pronouns *Pupil's Edition, p. 64*

1. To describe an action you do to yourself, use reflexive verbs (verbs ending in -**se**). The reflexive pronoun **se** can be used with the **él, ella, usted, ellos, ellas** and **ustedes** forms.

   Yo **me baño** a las ocho; luego mis hermanos **se bañan.**

   ¿A qué hora **te bañas** tú?

2. Place the reflexive pronoun before the conjugated verb or attached to an infinitive.

   Alfredo **se** baña a las siete, y luego le gusta afeitar**se.**

   Vamos a acostar**nos** a las once.

3. When using a reflexive verb with a part of the body, use a definite article.

   Se lava **los** dientes todos los días.

4 Natalia is describing her family's daily routine. Complete her description with the correct forms of the verbs in parentheses.

1. Mis padres _____ (despertarse) a las cinco.

2. Mi hermana y yo _____ (levantarse) a las siete y media.

3. Yo _____ (ducharse) y _____ (lavarse) el pelo a las ocho menos cuarto.

4. Luego mi hermano _____ (bañarse).

5. Uso una toalla pero mi hermano _____ (secarse) el pelo con la secadora de pelo.

6. Todos nosotros _____ (lavarse) los dientes todos los días.

5 Everyone in Lucita's family has a different routine. Complete her description with the correct forms of the verbs in parentheses.

Yo (1) _____ (levantarse) a las siete pero mis hermanos prefieren
(2) _____ (levantarse) a las ocho. A mi hermana le gusta
(3) _____ (bañarse) con agua fría. Yo (4) _____
(bañarse) con agua caliente. Los sábados mis hermanos quieren (5) _____
(despertarse) a las diez. Mi hermana y yo preferimos (6) _____
(despertarse) a las diez también. Mis padres (7) _____ (acostarse)
temprano. Y siempre me preguntan, "¿Por qué te gusta (8) _____
(acostarse) tan tarde?"

CAPÍTULO 3 Primer paso

Nota *G*ramatical   The verb **vestirse**   *Pupil's Edition, p. 65*

The reflexive verb **vestirse** *(to get dressed)* has the **e → i** stem change in all forms except **nosotros** and **vosotros**.

Primero mi esposa y yo **nos vestimos** y luego nuestros hijos **se visten**.

6 One of the actors in the school play is reviewing the times that people need to put on their costumes for scene changes in the evening performance. Complete each sentence with the correct form of **vestirse**.

1. Carlota y yo _____ a las seis y media.

2. Benjamín y Lupita _____ a las siete menos cuarto.

3. Alexa _____ a las siete menos cinco.

4. Yo _____ otra vez a las siete y diez.

5. David _____ a las siete y cuarto.

6. Y tú vas a _____ a las siete y cinco, ¿no?

Nota *G*ramatical   Adverbs   *Pupil's Edition, p. 66*

- Adverbs tell when things happen or how things are done.
- Many adverbs are formed by adding **-mente** to the feminine form of adjectives.
    sincero → **sinceramente**
- The suffix **-mente** is added to the end of adjectives that are the same in the masculine and feminine forms.
    normal → **normalmente**   constante → **constantemente**

7 Complete each sentence with an appropriate adverb based on an adjective in the word bank. You may make each sentence affirmative or negative.

constante   perfecto   elegante   triste
misterioso   rápido   horrible

1. Mi mejor amigo/a se viste _____ .

2. Yo canto _____ .

3. Mis amigos/as trabajan _____ .

4. Mi padre baila _____ .

5. Mis amigos y yo estudiamos _____ .

CAPÍTULO 3 Primer paso

■ SEGUNDO PASO

To talk about responsibilities, you'll often need to refer to household chores and use the direct object pronouns **lo, la, los,** and **las.** To make complaints, you'll need to use some new phrases.

¿Te acuerdas? Household chores   *Pupil's Edition, p. 68*

8 Complete the following sentences with the most appropriate words or expressions from the word bank.

> poner la mesa   tender la cama
> pasar la aspiradora   la cocina   cortar
>   barrer   la sala

1. Preparamos la comida en _____.

2. La primera cosa que hago después de levantarme es _____.

3. Cuando la alfombra está sucia, es necesario _____.

4. Antes de comer es necesario _____.

5. ¡Cuando llueve mucho tengo que _____ el césped tres veces por semana!

VOCABULARIO   More household chores   *Pupil's Edition, p. 68*

9 Imagine you're interviewing a young woman about her family's household routine. How would you ask . . . ?

1. if she straightens her room every day

   ¿ _____?

2. who takes out the garbage

   ¿ _____?

3. if her parents water the lawn on weekends

   ¿ _____?

4. if her father sets the table

   ¿ _____?

5. if her brothers or sisters clean the bathroom

   ¿ _____?

6. if she and her family make their beds

   ¿ _____?

CAPÍTULO 3 Segundo paso

*G*ramática   Direct object pronouns   *Pupil's Edition, p. 69*

The direct object pronouns **lo, la, los,** and **las** can take the place of direct object nouns in a sentence.

>¿Ya preparaste **la comida**?   Ya **la** preparé, sí.

1. Your choice of a direct object pronoun depends on the gender and number of the noun it replaces.

>¿Lavaste **el carro?**   Sí, **lo** lavé.

>¿Quién contestó **las preguntas**?   **Las** contestamos nosotros.

2. The direct object pronoun may be placed before the conjugated verb or may be attached to the infinitive.

>Allí está **la basura.**   ¿Vas a sacar**la**? or ¿**La** vas a sacar?

10 What would Alia's mother ask to find out if Alia did the following chores?

>MODELO   el cuarto de baño / limpiar
>**El cuarto de baño... ¿lo limpiaste?**

1. tu cuarto / ordenar _____

2. el césped / cortar _____

3. la mesa / quitar _____

4. los platos / lavar _____

5. la aspiradora / pasar _____

11 A friend is asking you some questions about who does certain chores at your house. Answer her questions, using direct object pronouns and the cues in parentheses.

>MODELO   En tu casa, ¿quién riega el jardín? (mi hermano)
>**Mi hermano lo riega.**

1. ¿Pones tú la mesa? (mi hermano y yo)

_____

2. ¿Quién va a lavar los platos esta noche? (mi papá)

_____

3. ¿Quién tiende las camas? (todos nosotros)

_____

4. ¿Quién va a barrer el piso esta semana? (yo)

_____

5. ¿Quién va a cortar el césped este fin de semana? (mi hermano)

_____

ASÍ SE DICE   Complaining   *Pupil's Edition, p. 70*

12 How might Nela respond in each situation to indicate that she thinks she's being treated unfairly? Use expressions from the phrase box.

> ¡No es justo!   Yo ya lo hice mil veces.   ¡Siempre me toca a mí!
>   Estoy harta de...   ¡Ay, qué pesado!

1. Her mother wants her to vacuum her bedroom, but she just spent two hours vacuuming.

   _____

2. She wishes somebody else would clear the dinner table, since she always has to do it.

   _____

3. Her father asks her to clean the bathroom, a chore that she really dislikes.

   _____

4. She feels like the chores aren't divided up fairly between her and her brother.

   _____

5. Her father asks her to answer the phone, which she's already done 10 times this morning.

   _____

13 Write a dialogue of six sentences in which Jon's father asks him to wash the car, clean the bathroom, and water the yard. Jon complains that he's already washed the car a thousand times, that he always has to clean the bathroom, and that it's not fair for him to water the yard because his sister never does it.

1. PAPÁ _____

   _____

2. JON _____

   _____

3. PAPÁ _____

   _____

4. JON _____

   _____

5. PAPÁ _____

   _____

6. JON _____

   _____

¡Ven conmigo! Level 2, Chapter 3   Grammar and Vocabulary Workbook, Teacher's Edition **23**

CAPÍTULO 3 Segundo paso

■ TERCER PASO

To talk about hobbies and pastimes, you'll need to use some new vocabulary. To say how long something has been going on, you'll need to use **hace** + *amount of time* + **que** + *present tense*.

VOCABULARIO Hobbies and pastimes *Pupil's Edition, p. 73*

14 Read the descriptions of the people in Column A and match each person with the hobby in Column B that he or she might like.

COLUMN A

_____ 1. Armando recibe cartas de muchos países.

_____ 2. Marisol toca dos instrumentos.

_____ 3. A Lorenzo le gusta estar con muchas personas.

_____ 4. A Amy le gusta la tecnología.

_____ 5. A Leah le gustan los carros.

COLUMN B

a. tocar con la banda

b. reunirse con los amigos

c. trabajar en mecánica

d. coleccionar estampillas

e. usar la computadora

15 Complete each statement with the correct phrases from the vocabulary of the **Tercer paso.** Conjugate verbs as necessary.

1. ¿Tienes problemas con tu carro? A mi amigo José le gusta mucho _____

_____.

2. Si te gusta la música puedes _____.

3. Mis abuelos _____
todas las noches porque les gustan los juegos de mesa.

4. A Diana le gusta mucho _____
todos los sábados en el Café Maya para hablar.

5. A Norberto le gustan los ejercicios aeróbicos. _____
todas las tardes después de sus clases.

16 Allison is answering questions from her new schoolmates about her hobbies. Supply the missing parts of their conversation.

MIGUEL (1) ¿_____?

ALLISON No, no tengo una colección de estampillas. Me gusta más estar con mis amigos.

ALEX (2) ¿_____?

ALLISON Me reúno todos los días con mis amigos, sí, después de clases.

ELENA (3) ¿_____?

ALLISON Durante el invierno, sí, mi familia y yo jugamos a las cartas.

MARTA (4) ¿_____?

ALLISON No, mis amigos no hacen monopatín. Prefieren usar la Internet en la computadora para hablar con gente de otras ciudades.

¿Te acuerdas? More hobbies and pastimes *Pupil's Edition, p. 73*

17 Javier is talking about his hobbies. Write the word or phrase that best completes each sentence.

1. Me gusta viajar y _____ con mi papá. Es más divertido que estar en un hotel.

   a. patinar   **b.** acampar   **c.** leer tiras cómicas

2. Voy mucho al lago para _____ con mis amigos.

   a. pescar   **b.** jugar videojuegos   **c.** leer tiras cómicas

3. Voy también al mar porque me gusta _____.

   a. patinar   **b.** leer tiras cómicas   **c.** bucear

4. En mis ratos libres voy a la librería a _____.

   a. acampar   **b.** patinar   **c.** leer tiras cómicas

5. Me interesan mucho las cosas electrónicas. Cada día después de mis clases,

   _____ y siempre gano.

   a. acampo   **b.** juego videojuegos   **c.** pesco

18 Víctor and his Colombian pen pal Inés are talking on the phone about their hobbies. Fill in the gaps in their conversation.

> VÍCTOR   **(1)** ¿ _____ ?
>
> INÉS   No, no toco con la banda pero me encanta la música. A ti te gustan los carros,
>
> ¿no? **(2)** ¿ _____ ?
>
> VÍCTOR   Sí, trabajo mucho en mecánica. Me fascinan los carros. En 20 años voy a tener
>
> una colección de carros de todos tipos.
>
> INÉS   **(3)** ¿ _____ ?
>
> VÍCTOR   No, no colecciono estampillas ni monedas. Sólo carros. A mí me gusta también
>
> estar cerca del agua. **(4)** ¿ _____ ?
>
> INÉS   No, no me gusta bucear pero pesco una o dos veces al mes. También me gusta
>
> mucho leer. **(5)** ¿ _____ ?
>
> VÍCTOR   ¡Sí, sí! Leo tiras cómicas todos los días. Me gustan en especial las tiras cómicas
>
> de Supergato.
>
> INÉS   **(6)** ¿ _____ ?
>
> VÍCTOR   Sí, me reúno mucho con mis amigos. ¡Me gustaría verte a ti en persona!

Nota *G*ramatical

Indicating how long something has been going on *Pupil's Edition, p. 74*

Use **hace** + *amount of time* + **que** + *present tense* to tell how long someone has been doing something.

    Hace tres años **que** vivo aquí. *I've lived here three years.*

19 Armando and Emily are talking about their pastimes. Complete their conversation with the correct words.

ARMANDO ¿Cuánto tiempo (1) _____ que haces monopatín?

EMILY (2) _____ tres o cuatro años que lo hago. Pero me gusta más bucear.

ARMANDO ¿Cuánto tiempo (3) _____ que buceas?

EMILY Hace cinco años (4) _____ buceo. ¿Buceas tú?

20 Entertainment reporter Rogelio Ferreter has just interviewed movie star Juanita Labarca. Based on his interview notes, write what he asked her, and then write her responses about how long she's been doing each thing listed below.

canta.........15 años	actriz.........5 años
poemas.........10 años	película..........4 semanas
Monterrey..........5 meses	guitarra.........10 años

MODELO cantar
    —¿Cuánto tiempo hace que usted canta?
    —Hace 15 años que canto.

1. ser actriz

  ¿ _____ ?

  _____

2. escribir poemas

  ¿ _____ ?

  _____

3. vivir en Monterrey

  ¿ _____ ?

  _____

CAPÍTULO 3 Tercer paso

¡Ven conmigo! Level 2, Chapter 3

CAPÍTULO 4

¡Adelante con los estudios!

PRIMER PASO

To give advice, you'll need to use **deberías, debes,** and vocabulary that describes things you should and shouldn't do at school. You may also need to use a variety of verbs and the preposition **para.**

Nota *G*ramatical **deberías** and **debes** *Pupil's Edition, p. 89*

You've already learned that **debes** means *you should*. If you want to give advice in a softer, less direct way, use **deberías.**

Deberías limpiar tu cuarto.

1 Zachary didn't do very well in school this semester. Imagine that you're his teacher and fill in the suggestions (**sugerencias**) section on his report card to help him do better next semester. Use **deberías** or **debes** and the verbs listed below.

estudiar las fechas importantes
leer los poemas antes de venir a clase
pintar una hora todos los días

saber los verbos irregulares
ir al laboratorio más frecuentemente

Colegio San Martín		
Estudiante: *Dylan, Zachary*		Grado 9
Materias	Nota	Sugerencias
Literatura	5	1. _____
Historia	4.6	2. _____
Inglés	6.9	3. _____
Química	7	4. _____
Arte	4.5	5. _____

VOCABULARIO   Things you should and   *Pupil's Edition, p. 89*
shouldn't do in school

2 Your committee is making a list of do's and don'ts to succeed in school. Complete each sentence with **Deberías** or **No deberías**.

1. _____ entregar la tarea todos los días.
2. _____ tomar apuntes en tus clases.
3. _____ suspender un examen o una clase.
4. _____ repasar tus apuntes antes del examen.
5. _____ hacer preguntas inteligentes en clase.

3 Choose a word from the word bank and write it by the definition it matches.

repasar   preocuparse   prestar atención   entregar la tarea
tomar apuntes   hacer preguntas

1. escuchar muy bien al profesor
2. escribir la información que la profesora presenta
3. estudiar el material otra vez antes de un examen
4. pedirle información al profesor
5. sentirse muy nervioso

4 Manuel and Manuela are twins, but they always do opposite things. Read what each twin does at school. Then describe what the other twin does, using verbs from the word bank.

prestar atención   dejar los libros en casa   entregar la tarea
aprobar los exámenes   sacar buenas notas

1. Manuela siempre suspende los exámenes de francés.

Manuel siempre _____ .
2. Manuel siempre trae su libro a la clase de álgebra.

Manuela siempre _____ .
3. Manuel siempre saca malas notas en la clase de historia.

Manuela siempre _____ .
4. Manuela siempre deja su tarea para la clase de biología en casa.

Manuel siempre _____ .
5. Manuel siempre duerme en la clase de arte.

Manuela siempre _____ .

VOCABULARIO More do's and don'ts for school *Pupil's Edition, p. 91*

5 Nothing Diego does on Mondays turns out right. Complete the following paragraph with the correct forms of the verbs in the word bank.

| aprender de memoria | copiar | olvidar | apuntar | perder |

Todos los lunes, Diego llega tarde a clase. Corre para tomar el autobús

pero siempre lo **(1)** _____. Siempre

(2) _____ sus libros porque tiene sueño. Y suspende

los exámenes porque no **(3)** _____ las nuevas palabras.

Siempre da la misma explicación: "No **(4)** _____ la fecha

del examen en mi cuaderno"; por eso durante el almuerzo Diego tiene que

(5) _____ los apuntes de un amigo. ¡Nunca aprende de

sus errores!

¿Te acuerdas? The preposition **para** *Pupil's Edition, p. 91*

Para means *in order to* when followed by a verb. The verb will always be in the infinitive form.

6 Create sentences to find out what people do to excel in class.

1. mucho / sacar / para / notas / Michelle / estudia / buenas

   _____

2. para / el vocabulario / Andreas y Lew / aprenderlo de memoria / repiten

   _____

3. Megan y yo / buenos apuntes / tomar / escuchamos bien / para

   _____

7 Using the cues, write five sentences about learning from the Internet.

1. **navegar por la red** _____

2. **el Internet** _____

3. **la página Web** _____

4. **el correo electrónico** _____

5. **la Telaraña Mundial** _____

■ SEGUNDO PASO

To talk about things and people you know, you'll need to use adjectives and the verbs **ser** and **estar**. You'll also need to use the verb **conocer**. To make comparisons, you'll need to use **más** and **menos**.

VOCABULARIO   Adjectives used to describe people   *Pupil's Edition, p. 93*

8 Some people believe opposites attract. With this in mind, match each person in Column A with his or her best friend in Column B. One sentence in Column B will not be used.

COLUMN A

_____ 1. Rubén nunca olvida nada.

_____ 2. María es muy atlética.

_____ 3. Alejo es bastante flojo.

_____ 4. El señor Lugones no es muy estricto.

COLUMN B

a. Susana es un poco torpe.

b. Esteban es muy distraído.

c. Karla es muy justa.

d. Don Simón es muy exigente.

e. Ana es una estudiante aplicada.

Nota *G*ramatical   The verb **ser** with adjectives   *Pupil's Edition, p. 93*

- Use **ser** + *adjective* to describe someone's physical traits and personality.
  Antonio **es** alto y simpático.
- Use **ser** + *adjective of nationality* to describe someone's nationality.
  Don Luis y su esposa **son** cubanos.

9 Vonna is describing a few people at school to a new exchange student. Complete her sentences with the correct forms of **ser.**

Virginia **(1)** _____ cubana y **(2)** _____ muy creativa. Pinta todos los días y sabe tocar el piano. Pero a Antonio y a mí no nos gusta trabajar como a Virginia. Nosotros **(3)** _____ un poco flojos. Mi hermana Margarita y su amigo Enrique **(4)** _____ muy responsables. Siempre llegan a clase a tiempo y estudian todos los días. Hishem y Denise también **(5)** _____ muy aplicados. Ellos están en el laboratorio de química hasta las seis de la tarde todos los días. Carlos **(6)** _____ muy atlético . . . corre cinco millas por la mañana y por la tarde nada con el equipo del colegio. Y todos dicen que tú **(7)** _____ muy entusiasta en todas tus clases. Dicen que contestas muchas preguntas en clase y que quieres participar en las actividades del colegio. Pero yo no voy a cambiar . . . voy a **(8)** _____ floja siempre. ¿Qué te puedo decir?

Copyright © by Holt, Rinehart and Winston. All rights reserved.

10 Several teachers are discussing their students' strengths and weaknesses. Write descriptions of the students they mention, using the correct forms of **ser** and appropriate adjectives from the word bank.

flojo	creativo	distraído	generoso	honesto

MODELO   Judith nunca quiere trabajar.   **Es bastante floja.**

1. Amalia tiene muchas ideas originales. _____

2. Toni y Dan siempre ayudan a sus compañeros con la tarea. _____

3. Ben siempre deja su tarea en casa. _____

4. Beto y Ana siempre dicen la verdad. _____

11 Pablo is putting together a list of the exchange students at his school. Based on the clues given, write a sentence indicating each person's national or regional origin.

MODELO   Alejandro / España   **Alejandro es español.**

1. Yo / Costa Rica _____

2. José Luis y Paca / México _____

3. Tú / Chile _____

4. Eleanora / Cuba _____

5. Todos nosotros / las Américas _____

Nota *G*ramatical   The verb **estar** with adjectives   *Pupil's Edition, p. 93*

Use **estar** to tell where something is located, to describe how someone feels, or to describe states or conditions.

Matthew **está** enfermo y no puede venir a clase.

12 Complete Úrsula's diary entry using the correct forms of **estar**.

5 de octubre
Yo siempre (1) _____ contenta cuando mi amigo Rafael y yo
(2) _____ juntos. Pero hoy yo (3) _____
triste porque Rafael (4) _____ en el hospital. Sus padres
(5) _____ con él en el hospital. Yo (6) _____
preocupada por él.

13 Write a sentence describing each situation below, using **estar** and the appropriate adjective from the word bank.

| aburrido | tranquilo | preocupado | ocupado | emocionado |

1. Yo tengo que copiar mis apuntes para la clase de álgebra, estudiar para el examen de historia y escribir tres composiciones para la clase de inglés.

   Yo _____ .

2. Tú no puedes encontrar a tu perro. Hace tres días que lo buscas.

   Tú _____ .

3. Marisol y yo no tenemos nada que hacer y no hay nada bueno en la televisión.

   Marisol y yo _____ .

4. Mañana es la Navidad y los niños no pueden dormir porque quieren abrir sus regalos.

   Los niños _____ .

14 Margarita is writing a note about her English class to her friend Heidi. Complete her note with the correct forms of **ser** or **estar**.

> Es la primera semana de clases y yo (1) _____ cansada. Tengo siete clases al día. El profesor de inglés (2) _____ estadounidense y (3) _____ muy exigente. Muchos estudiantes en la clase (4) _____ enfadados porque nos da mucha tarea. Pero prefiero (5) _____ ocupada. No me gusta (6) _____ aburrida.
>
> Hasta pronto,
> Margarita

15 Write sentences about yourself and people you know, using **ser** or **estar** and the adjectives in parentheses. Your sentences may be positive or negative.

1. (alto) _____

2. (preocupado) _____

3. (ocupado) _____

4. (enfermo) _____

5. (inteligente) _____

6. (emocionado) _____

7. (triste) _____

Nota *G*ramatical   The verb **conocer**   *Pupil's Edition, p. 94*

Use the verb **conocer** to say that you know someone or that you are familiar with a place. Be sure to use **a** after **conocer** when talking about people.
   ¿Conocen ustedes **a** mi tía Mariana?

16 Answer the questions using complete sentences and the correct form of **conocer**.

1. ¿Conoces a la nueva profesora de computación?

   No, _____ .

2. Mateo viene de Detroit mañana para vacaciones. ¿Conoce Gaby a Mateo?

   Sí, _____ .

3. ¿Conocen ustedes ese restaurante que está en la calle Hudson? Tiene comida buena.

   Sí, _____ .

4. Tus amigos van a llegar este fin de semana, ¿verdad? ¿Conocen México?

   No, _____ .

¿Te acuerdas?   Comparisons of inequality   *Pupil's Edition, p. 95*

To compare people, places, and things that are different, use **más . . . que** or **menos . . . que**.

17 Compare the following people and things using the adjectives in parentheses.

MODELO   Bárbara estudia todos los días pero Carmen nunca estudia. (aplicado)
             Bárbara **es más aplicada que Carmen.**

1. La profesora Chen nos da poca tarea pero la profesora Slawsky nos da mucha. (exigente)

   La profesora Slawsky _____ .

2. Ricardo mide dos metros y Rudolfo mide un metro cincuenta. (alto)

   Rudolfo _____ .

3. Las zapatillas de Elvira cuestan cincuenta dólares y las zapatillas de Michelle cuestan cuarenta. (caro)

   Las zapatillas de Michelle _____ .

4. Paquita siempre trae su libro a clase pero Josefina siempre lo deja en casa. (distraído)

   Josefina _____ .

5. Li hace todos los ejercicios del libro pero Mona sólo hace los ejercicios fáciles. (flojo)

   Mona _____ .

■ TERCER PASO

In order to make plans, you'll need to talk about everyday activities. You'll also need to use direct object pronouns.

VOCABULARIO   Everyday activities   *Pupil's Edition, p. 98*

18 Mr. Obregón is telling you about his family's hectic schedule. Complete each sentence with the correct form of the most logical item from the word bank.

> platicar   ir a una cita   merendar   hacer cola   mirar las vitrinas
> tomar el metro   reunirse con sus amigas

1. Para ir al partido los domingos mi hijo y yo _____ al Estadio Maya.

2. El martes mi hija _____ con el dentista.

3. Los miércoles mi esposa _____ para platicar.

4. Mi esposa _____ de las tiendas en el Centro Comercial Siglo XXI los jueves.

5. Los viernes mi esposa y sus amigas _____ en el café.

6. Luego mi esposa va a casa de sus papás para _____ con ellos de las actividades de nuestros hijos.

7. Y los sábados yo _____ en el Cine Vanguardia y compro boletos para mi familia.

---

*G*ramática   Direct object pronouns   *Pupil's Edition, p. 100*

You have already learned how to use the direct object pronouns **lo, los, la,** and **las.** The pronouns **me, te,** and **nos** refer to *me, you* (informal), and *us.* Remember to put object pronouns directly before the conjugated verb or to attach them to the infinitive.

  Necesito levantar este sofá. ¿**Me** puedes ayudar? No puedo levantar**lo** solo.

---

19 Write the direct object pronoun that would take the place of these words.

_____ 1. mi madre   _____ 6. los sombreros

_____ 2. las computadoras _____ 7. la casa

_____ 3. nosotras   _____ 8. tú

_____ 4. yo   _____ 9. tu padre

_____ 5. el problema   _____ 10. la ensalada

¡Ven conmigo! Level 2, Chapter 3

20 Imagine you're planning a party with a friend. Use the correct direct object pronoun for the underlined object in the answers.

MODELO   ¿Compraste la comida?

Sí, **la compré.**

1. ¿<u>Me</u> puedes ayudar con las decoraciones?

Sí, _____ .

2. ¿<u>Te</u> puedo llamar esta tarde a las siete?

No, no _____ .

3. ¿Vas a comprar <u>los refrescos</u> esta tarde?

Sí, _____ .

4. ¿Mandaste <u>las invitaciones</u> hoy?

No, no _____ .

5. Lola y Juan vienen mañana. ¿<u>Nos</u> llamas a las ocho?

Sí, _____ .

6. Necesitamos música. ¿Tienes mi <u>radio</u>?

No, no _____ .

21 Write answers in Spanish to the following questions about your everyday activities. Use direct object pronouns in your responses.

1. ¿Miras mucho las vitrinas?

_____

_____

2. ¿Vas a mirar las vitrinas este fin de semana?

_____

_____

3. ¿Tomas el metro a la escuela?

_____

_____

4. ¿Siempre apruebas los exámenes de español?

_____

_____

5. ¿Quieres ver la película el domingo?

_____

_____

Nombre _____ Clase _____ Fecha _____

¡Ponte en forma!

■ PRIMER PASO

To talk about staying fit and healthy, you'll need to know the names of outdoor activities and of things people do at the gym. You'll also need to use the preterite tense.

VOCABULARIO   Outdoor activities   *Pupil's Edition, p. 117*

1 Juliana is playing a guessing game about outdoor activities with her little brother. Write the activity that corresponds to each sentence.

1. Debes hacerlo antes y después de correr. _____

2. Es el acto de nadar. _____

3. Lo haces en una canoa. _____

4. Es el acto de caminar, generalmente en el campo. _____

5. Es el acto de escalar montañas. _____

6. Lo haces en una bicicleta. _____

2 Read the following advertisement for a youth fitness camp, and fill in the blanks with the appropriate vocabulary words.

Campamento Monte Saldívar
Deportes / Recreo
Tels. 555-34-47, 555-34-48

¿Quieres ponerte en forma? ¿Buscas oportunidades de recreo?
¡Debes visitar nuestro campamento!

Hay algo para todos en el Campamento Monte Saldívar. Si te gusta el

(1) _____, tenemos un río super bonito. Si prefieres la

(2) _____, hay una piscina de tipo olímpico. ¿Te gusta el

(3) _____? Tenemos lugares bonitos por donde caminar. ¿Tienes

bicicleta? Nuestro campamento es ideal para el **(4)** _____. Y si te

interesa **(5)** _____ montañas, tenemos unas montañas espectaculares.

  El Campamento Monte Saldívar... no debes perdértelo.

Nota *G*ramatical   The verb **dormir** in the preterite   *Pupil's Edition, p. 118*

Dormir *(to sleep)* is irregular in the third-person singular and plural forms of the preterite.

yo dormí	nosotros dormimos
tú dormiste	vosotros dormisteis
él / ella / usted d<u>u</u>rmió	ellos / ellas / ustedes d<u>u</u>rmieron

3 Lourdes is a counselor at a summer camp. Help her find out how well her campers slept by completing the following conversation with the correct forms of **dormir**.

LOURDES   ¿Ustedes (1) _____ bien anoche?

TRACI y LUISITA   Sí, (2) _____ siete horas y media.

LOURDES   Y tú, Lara, ¿cuántas horas (3) _____?

LARA   No sé exactamente. La verdad es que no (4) _____ muy

bien. Tres horas, más o menos.

LOURDES   Lo siento. Debe usted hablar con la enfermera esta tarde. Y tú, Megan,

¿(5) _____ bien?

MEGAN   Sí, yo (6) _____ bien, ¡pero Lara dice que yo ronqué

(snored) toda la noche!

VOCABULARIO   At the gym   *Pupil's Edition, p. 119*

4 Write the word or phrase that best completes each sentence.

1. Norberto come muchas verduras porque quiere _____.
   a. bajar de peso   **b.** aumentar de peso   **c.** moverse

2. Gloria no tiene pesas en casa. Va a _____.
   a. bajar de peso   **b.** inscribirse en un gimnasio   **c.** sudar

3. Claudine está tomando una clase de ejercicios aeróbicos porque le gusta

   _____.
   a. levantar pesas   **b.** inscribirse en el gimnasio   **c.** moverse

4. Para bajar de peso, Helena _____ en casa.
   a. salta a la cuerda   **b.** aumenta de peso   **c.** se inscribe en el gimnasio

5. Steffi _____ porque quiere poder defenderse.
   a. hace abdominales   **b.** baja de peso   **c.** practica las artes marciales

6. Casey _____ mucho en su clase de ejercicios aeróbicos.
   a. levanta pesas   **b.** se mueve   **c.** practica las artes marciales

CAPÍTULO 5 Primer paso

5 Diego is talking to you about what he and his friends do to stay fit and healthy. Complete his sentences with the correct present-tense forms of the verbs in the word bank. Not all the verbs will be used.

| bajar | saltar | hacer | inscribirse | levantar | practicar |

1. A mí me gusta _____ a la cuerda.

2. Mi amigo Néstor _____ abdominales y a veces él y yo

   _____ pesas juntos.

3. Creo que Emilia y Beth _____ las artes marciales en el gimnasio los jueves.

4. Jaime quiere ir al nuevo gimnasio. _____ allí hoy.

Gramática   Preterite of -**er** and -**ir** verbs   *Pupil's Edition, p. 120*

1. Both -**er** and -**ir** verbs have the same endings in the preterite tense.

COMER		ESCRIBIR	
comí	comimos	escribí	escribimos
comiste	comisteis	escribiste	escribisteis
comió	comieron	escribió	escribieron

2. The forms of **dar** *(to give)* in the preterite are **di, diste, dio, dimos,** disteis, and **dieron.**

6 Write the correct preterite form of each verb according to the subjects provided.

1. él / correr _____
2. nosotros / escribir _____
3. tú / asistir _____
4. ellos / sorprender _____
5. ellos / dar _____
6. yo / salir _____
7. Alicia y yo / perder _____
8. usted / dar _____
9. Berta / sacudir _____
10. tú / tender _____

7 Answer the questions about what people did last week to keep fit using the cues in parentheses.

1. ¿Cuántas millas corriste? (tres)

   _____

2. ¿Cuándo se inscribió Rafael en un gimnasio? (el jueves pasado)

   _____

3. ¿Cuándo asistieron ustedes a la clase de ejercicios aeróbicos? (anoche)

   _____

4. ¿Qué comió Mikaela para evitar la grasa? (muchas verduras)

   _____

¿Se te ha olvidado?   Preterite of -ar verbs   *Pupil's Edition, p. 120*

8 Tom is talking to his grandmother about what he and his family did last weekend. Complete each sentence with the correct preterite form of the verb in parentheses.

1. Abuelita, el sábado un amigo y yo _____ (levantar) pesas en el gimnasio.

2. Mi amigo no _____ (sudar) mucho pero yo sí.

3. Alicia _____ (practicar) las artes marciales en el parque con el club de la escuela.

4. Yo _____ (escalar) una montaña con mis amigos.

5. Y mamá y papá _____ (saltar) a la cuerda porque quieren bajar de peso.

6. Y tú, abuelita, ¿_____ (caminar) ayer con mi abuelito?

9 Marion and her friend Pam went on vacation together but didn't do the same things. Based on their to-do lists, write sentences in which Marion tells what she did, what Pam did, and what they both did.

Marion	*Pam*
remar en el Río Piedras	nadar ✔
escalar la Montaña Brava ✔	dar una caminata por el Parque Nacional ✔
nadar ✔	escalar la Montaña Brava
dormir 10 horas todos los días ✔	remar en el Río Piedras ✔
escribir cartas a mi familia ✔	escribir cartas a mi familia ✔
dar una caminata por el Parque Nacional ✔	dormir 10 horas todos los días

MODELO   **Yo escalé la Montaña Brava pero Pam no la escaló.**

1. _____

_____

2. _____

_____

3. _____

_____

4. _____

CAPÍTULO 5 Primer paso

■ SEGUNDO PASO

To tell someone what to do and not to do, you might want to use some health-related vocabulary, as well as regular and irregular informal commands.

VOCABULARIO   Good health habits   *Pupil's Edition, p. 123*

10 Complete the following gym advertisement with the appropriate vocabulary words.

Gimnasio El Universal
Avenida Ingenieros No. 137
Tel. 332-47-48

¿Quieres mantenerte en **(1)** _____? ¿Necesitas entrenarte para

una **(2)** _____? ¿Necesitas **(3)** _____ más

tiempo a tu **(4)** _____ personal? ¿Quieres aprender buenos

(5) _____ de salud? Si respondiste «Sí» a una de estas

preguntas, tenemos el gimnasio perfecto para ti. Si quieres levantar pesas,

aprender a evitar la **(6)** _____, o tomar clases de ejercicio

aeróbico, El Universal es TU GIMNASIO.

---

11 Adolfo filled out a questionnaire at the doctor's office. Based on his responses, write the questions that appeared on the questionnaire.

Clínica Buendía
Calle Otavalo 36

1. ¿ _____ ?
   Sí, creo que necesito hacer régimen.

2. ¿ _____ ?
   Sí, evito la grasa. Pero creo que como demasiado a veces.

3. ¿ _____ ?
   No, no puedo respirar profundamente después de hacer ejercicios aeróbicos.

4. ¿ _____ ?
   Sí, me relajo después de hacer ejercicio pero no hago suficiente ejercicio.

5. ¿ _____ ?
   Sí, necesito reducir el estrés en mi vida. ¿Cómo lo puedo hacer?

---

*G*ramática   Informal commands   *Pupil's Edition, p. 123*

Use informal commands to tell a friend or a child to do something.

1. To create affirmative informal commands, drop the **-s** ending of the **tú** form of the verb.

STATEMENT	COMMAND
(tú) estudia**s**	¡Estudi**a**!
(tú) come**s**	¡Com**e**!
(tú) piensa**s**	¡Piens**a**!

2. To form negative **tú** commands, change the **-as** ending in **-ar** verbs to **-es** and the **-es** ending in **-er** verbs to **-as**. Place the **no** before the verb and also before reflexive pronouns.

STATEMENT	COMMAND
(tú) camin**as**	¡No camin**es**!
(tú) duerm**es**	¡No duerm**as**!

12 Nikki wants to learn better health habits. Use affirmative or negative commands, as appropriate, to give her advice.

MODELO   comer muchos postres
    No comas muchos postres.

1. evitar la grasa

   _____

2. tomar mucha agua cada día

   _____

3. trabajar todo el tiempo

   _____

4. caminar un poco cada día

   _____

5. comer sólo carne

   _____

6. respirar profundamente cuando haces ejercicio

   _____

7. dormir ocho horas todas las noches

   _____

8. beber refrescos todo el tiempo

   _____

9. correr largas distancias si no corres frecuentemente

   _____

CAPÍTULO 5 Segundo paso

Nota Gramatical
Negative command forms of -**gar** and -**car** verbs   *Pupil's Edition, p. 124*

- The negative command forms of verbs that end in -**gar** are spelled with **gu** instead of **g** to preserve the hard *g* sound.

    jugar → No jue**gu**es al tenis después de comer.

- The negative command forms of verbs that end in -**car** change the **c** to **qu** in order to preserve the *k* sound.

    dedicar → No dedi**qu**es todo tu tiempo al trabajo.

13 Fill in the blanks with the correct negative command forms of the verbs in parentheses.

1. _____ (sacar) malas notas... estudia todos los días.

2. _____ (practicar) deportes cuando debes estudiar.

3. _____ (llegar) tarde a tus clases.

4. Y _____ (entregar) tu tarea tarde.

Gramática
Irregular informal commands   *Pupil's Edition, p. 124*

Some verbs have irregular informal command forms. The affirmative and negative command forms of these verbs are shown below.

Infinitive	Aff.	Neg.	Infinitive	Aff.	Neg.
hacer	**haz**	no **hagas**	ser	**sé**	no **seas**
poner	**pon**	no **pongas**	venir	**ven**	no **vengas**
tener	**ten**	no **tengas**	salir	**sal**	no **salgas**
ir	**ve**	no **vayas**	decir	**di**	no **digas**

14 Write advice for someone with health concerns, using affirmative or negative informal commands as appropriate.

MODELO   venir al gimnasio conmigo   **Ven al gimnasio conmigo.**

1. ir a clases de ejercicios aeróbicos

_____

2. ponerle sal a la comida

_____

3. hacer abdominales todos los días

_____

4. decirle adiós a la grasa

_____

5. ser flojo en tu régimen

_____

■ TERCER PASO

In order to make excuses, you may want to use **poder** in the preterite and some vocabulary that refers to parts of the body and to aches and pains.

Nota *G*ramatical   The preterite of **poder**   *Pupil's Edition, p. 128*

Poder *(to be able; can)* is irregular in the preterite tense.

yo **pude**	nosotros **pudimos**
tú **pudiste**	vosotros pudisteis
él / ella / usted **pudo**	ellos / ellas / ustedes **pudieron**

---

15 Kendra is talking to you about what she and her family were able to accomplish last weekend. Complete each sentence with the correct preterite form of **poder.**

1. Yo _____ hacer toda mi tarea.

2. Mi hermana y yo _____ remar un poco en el río.

3. Mi papá _____ inscribirse en el gimnasio.

4. Mi mamá y mi hermano _____ escribir unas cartas.

5. Y, ¿qué _____ hacer tú?

VOCABULARIO   The body   *Pupil's Edition, p. 129*

16 Write the word in each list that doesn't belong.

_____ 1. el codo, el dedo, la nariz, la muñeca, el hombro

_____ 2. el muslo, la cabeza, el cuello, los ojos, la nariz

_____ 3. la rodilla, la pantorrilla, el tobillo, el muslo, el cuello

_____ 4. hacerse daño, lastimarse, relajarse, doler, tener calambre

17 Read the following pieces of conversations that a sports doctor had with his patients. Fill in the gaps, using words from the vocabulary on page 129 of your textbook.

DR. VALENCIA   (1) ¿ _____ el hombro, Gaby?

GABY   Sí, Dr. Valencia, me duele muchísimo y no puedo mover el brazo.

DR. VALENCIA   Manolo, (2) ¿ _____ el tobillo?

MANOLO   Sí, doctor, me lo torcí y me duele mucho.

DR. VALENCIA   Andrés, (3) ¿ _____ la pantorrilla?

ANDRÉS   No, doctor, no me lastimé la pantorrilla. Me lastimé el muslo.

DR. VALENCIA   Daniela, (4) ¿ _____ en el muslo?

DANIELA   Sí, tengo calambre en el muslo, doctor. ¿Qué debo hacer?

VOCABULARIO   Reflexive verbs   *Pupil's Edition, p. 130*

18 Fill in the blanks in Laura's e-mail message with the correct preterite forms of verbs from the word bank.

| quejarse | divertirse | cansarse | enfermarse | acordarse | olvidarse |

Sheri, la fiesta en casa de Maribel fue horrible. Yo no

(1) _____ . La fiesta empezó mal porque Álvaro

(2) _____ de preparar los sándwiches. Por eso

fue al supermercado a comprar sándwiches. Ignacio comió uno y

(3) _____ . Se fue a casa con dolor de estómago.

Luego escuchamos un disco compacto de "Los Locos" pero Katrina y

Andrew **(4)** _____ de la música porque no les gusta

el grupo. Bailamos pero después de 30 minutos todos nosotros

(5) _____ de bailar. ¡Qué bueno que tú no fuiste!

Laura

Nota Gramatical   Reflexive verbs that *Pupil's Edition, p. 130* express feelings

Some reflexive verbs can be used to express feelings.

Me enfermé porque comí demasiado.

19 Complete the following sentences about you, your family, and your friends by writing the correct forms of the verbs in parentheses and adding other words.

MODELO   Yo **me divierto** (divertirse) cuando **remo en el Río Robledo.**

1. Mis amigos y yo _____ (divertirse) mucho cuando _____

_____ .

2. A veces yo _____ (enfermarse) cuando _____

_____ .

3. Mi mejor amigo/a nunca _____ (cansarse) cuando _____

_____ .

4. Mis padres _____ (quejarse) cuando yo _____

_____ .

CAPÍTULO 6

De visita en la ciudad

■ PRIMER PASO

To ask for and give information, you'll need to refer to places around town. You'll also need to use the verbs **saber** and **conocer**.

VOCABULARIO   Places around town   *Pupil's Edition, p. 143*

1 Complete each definition with the correct word from the word bank.

turista	se sube	letrero	conductor	semáforo	iglesia	se baja

1. Cuando una persona entra en el autobús se dice que "_____ al autobús".

2. Cuando una persona sale del autobús se dice que "_____ del autobús".

3. El _____ es algo que ayuda a controlar *(control)* el tráfico.

4. Una persona que visita los lugares de interés se llama un _____ .

5. Una persona que maneja un autobús es un _____ .

6. Puedes leer el _____ si necesitas información.

2 Use the clues to tell where Herminia is at various times of the day.

el edificio	el semáforo	el puente	la parada del autobús	el río	la iglesia

MODELO   9:00   Está dejando su coche.
   A las nueve está en el estacionamiento.

1. 9:30   Está esperando el autobús.

_____

2. 10:00   Está hablando con el agente de viajes en su oficina.

_____

3. 1:00   Está asistiendo a una boda.

_____

4. 2:00   Está cruzando *(crossing)* el río.

_____

5. 5:00   Está mirando la ciudad desde *(from)* una lancha.

_____

Nota Gramatical — The present tense of saber *Pupil's Edition, p. 144*

Here is the present tense of **saber**: **sé, sabes, sabe, sabemos,** sabéis, **saben.**

3 Complete Humberto's conversation with the correct forms of **saber.**

HUMBERTO Perdone, ¿(1) _____ usted dónde está la oficina de turismo?

SRA. PONCE No, yo no (2) _____, pero pregúntales a esos señores allá.

HUMBERTO ¿(3) _____ ustedes cómo se va a la oficina de turismo?

SR. ÁLVAREZ Sí, claro, nosotros (4) _____ muy bien dónde está la oficina de turismo. Está en la calle Market. Debes hablar con la señora Hidalgo.

Ella (5) _____ hablar español y te puede ayudar mucho.

4 Cecilia is presenting the results of a survey of what her classmates know about San Antonio. Complete her sentences with the correct forms of **saber.**

1. Yo / que San Antonio está en Texas

_____

2. Alicia y yo / que muchos turistas visitan San Antonio

_____

3. Fernando / que muchas personas hablan español allí

_____

4. Paco y Luisa / dónde está el Álamo

_____

5. Loretha / que hay partidos de fútbol en el Álamodome

_____

5 Beatriz works in a tourist office in San Antonio. Based on her responses, write the questions these tourists are asking her. Be sure to use the verb **saber.**

SR. LÓPEZ (1) ¿ _____?

BEATRIZ No, señor, no sé dónde está el restaurante Finni.

SRA. ARGENSOLA (2) ¿ _____?

BEATRIZ Sí, sé muy bien dónde puede comprar vestidos bonitos. ¡En La Villita!

SR. DELIBES (3) ¿ _____?

BEATRIZ Sí, sabemos mucho sobre la historia de San Antonio.

SRTA. JAMES (4) ¿ _____?

BEATRIZ Sí, sé cuándo fundaron *(they founded)* la misión San José. La fundaron en 1720.

Gramática saber vs. conocer *Pupil's Edition, p. 145*

Both **saber** and **conocer** mean *to know,* but they are used in different circumstances.
- **Saber** means *to know* facts or information.
    María no **sabe** dónde está el Álamo.
- When followed by an infinitive, **saber** means *to know how to do something.*
    ¿**Sabes** jugar al tenis?
- **Conocer** means *to know* or *to be acquainted with* a person or a place.
    ¿**Conoce** usted el Paseo del Río?
- Remember to use the personal **a** with people after **conocer**.
    ¿No **conoces a** Marta?

6 José Antonio is a Chilean exchange student living in Texas. Complete his letter to his mother with the correct forms of **conocer** or **saber**.

Me encanta Texas. Hace sólo un mes que estoy aquí, pero ya

(1) _____ a muchas personas. Mi familia tejana

(2) _____ mucho de la historia de Texas y ellos

(3) _____ un millón de lugares super interesantes.

Voy este fin de semana a San Antonio con mi amigo Marc. Él

(4) _____ a dos chicas de allí y ellas

(5) _____ un parque nacional donde se puede bajar el

río en canoa. Mamá, ¿(6) _____ tú que en Texas comen

mermelada de jalapeño? Si quieres te mando un poco.

7 How would you express the following things in Spanish?

1. You'd like to ask your friend if he or she is familiar with the **Paseo del Río**.

    ¿ _____?

2. You'd like to ask your friends if they know some teachers in San Antonio.

    ¿ _____?

3. You'd like to ask your friends if they are familiar with **la Torre de las Américas**.

    ¿ _____?

4. You'd like to ask your friend's parents if they know where **el Álamodome** is.

    ¿ _____?

5. You'd like to ask your teacher if he or she is familiar with the **Misión San José**.

    ¿ _____?

CAPÍTULO 6 Primer Paso

■ SEGUNDO PASO

To relate a series of events that happened in the past, you'll need to use the preterite tense. You'll also need to refer to places you went and things you saw and did.

VOCABULARIO   Sightseeing and travel   *Pupil's Edition, pp. 147, 149*

8 Use the following clues to solve the crossword puzzle.

Horizontales

1. persona que viaja en un tren o avión
5. tipo de boleto que te permite ir a un lugar y regresar a casa (cuatro palabras)
7. persona que te lleva el equipaje

Verticales

2. lugar donde esperas el tren
3. el _____ botánico, lugar donde puedes ver plantas exóticas
4. otra palabra para **viaje**
6. lugar muy alto donde puedes ver toda la ciudad

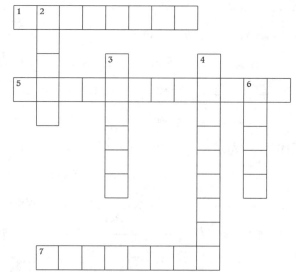

9 Fill in the blanks in this conversation with the correct vocabulary words.

COLIN   Estoy muy emocionado porque acabo de comprar mi boleto de **(1)** _____

y _____ a Austin. Tengo que estar en la **(2)** _____ de tren a las siete de la mañana.

CASSIE   ¿Con quién viajas?

COLIN   Bueno, voy a encontrar a mis tíos en el **(3)** _____ a las siete y cuarto y todos viajamos juntos.

CASSIE   ¿Y qué piensas hacer en Austin?

COLIN   Creo que vamos al Parque Zilker para ver las flores bonitas en el **(4)** _____

_____ que tienen allí. Y después vamos a la Universidad de Texas.

CASSIE   La universidad tiene una **(5)** _____ muy alta, ¿no?

COLIN   Creo que sí. ¡Qué ganas tengo de ir!

ASÍ SE DICE   Relating a series of events   *Pupil's Edition, p. 148*

10 Constance is telling you, in order, what she and her sisters did yesterday. Complete her sentences with appropriate vocabulary items from the word bank.

Luego	A continuación	Por último	Primero	Después

1. _____ yo llamé a mi abuelito.

2. _____ mi hermana Kerry y yo escuchamos unos discos compactos.

3. _____ Kerry y mi otra hermana Marcie corrieron en el parque.

4. _____ Kerry se bañó y fue al cine.

5. _____ estudiamos para nuestras clases y nos acostamos.

¿Te acuerdas?   The preterite   *Pupil's Edition, p. 148*

- Use the preterite to list a series of actions completed in the past.
- The preterite endings for regular -**ar**, -**er**, and -**ir** verbs are as follows:

-AR		-ER and -IR	
nadé	nadamos	comí	comimos
nadaste	nadasteis	comiste	comisteis
nadó	nadaron	comió	comieron

---

11 Aurelia is talking about what she and her family did on the first day of their vacation. Fill in the blanks with the correct preterite forms of the verbs in parentheses.

Nosotros **(1)** _____ (llegar) al hotel a las diez de la mañana. Mis padres

(2) _____ (descansar) allí hasta el mediodía. Mis hermanas Lidia y

Anastasia **(3)** _____ (mirar) una película a la una y después nosotros

(4) _____ (ir) al parque de atracciones. Nos **(5)** _____

(gustar) mucho el parque y nos **(6)** _____ (divertir) mucho allí. Mis

padres **(7)** _____ (comprar) algunas cosas en el centro comercial a

las cinco y luego nosotros **(8)** _____ (ir) al mejor restaurante de

la ciudad, El Sol Azteca. Nos **(9)** _____ (encantar) el lugar. Yo

(10) _____ (comer) las mejores enchiladas del mundo. ¡Tienes que

visitarlo algún día! Por último nosotros **(11)** _____ (regresar) al hotel.

CAPÍTULO 6 Segundo Paso

12 What did these people do last Saturday? Write sentences using the preterite and appropriate expressions from the word bank.

MODELO Mary: ir a la playa / mirar una película / escribir unas cartas

Primero, Mary fue a la playa. Después miró una película y por último escribió unas cartas.

primero	a continuación	después	luego	por último

1. Alan y yo: ir a un partido de fútbol / visitar el jardín botánico / salir con nuestros amigos

_____

_____

_____

2. Chad: mirar una película / comprar unos discos compactos nuevos / llamar a su abuela

_____

_____

_____

13 Phil made some notes about the day he just spent with his grandparents in south Texas. Based on his notes, write his description of what he and his grandparents did, using the preterite and expressions from **Así se dice** on page 148 of your textbook.

	10:00	Yo — comprar regalos para mi familia
	10:30	abuelita — caminar en el parque Bentsen
	1:00	abuelos — descansar
	2:00	abuelito y yo — ir a Reynosa
	7:00	abuelos y yo — comer en un restaurante mexicano

_____

_____

_____

_____

_____

_____

_____

■ TERCER PASO

To order in a restaurant, you'll need to use restaurant vocabulary as well as the preterite of the verbs **pedir**, **servir**, and **traer**.

VOCABULARIO   Restaurant vocabulary   *Pupil's Edition, p. 153*

14 Read each definition and rewrite the scrambled words in the correct order.

_____ 1. Es el hombre que sirve la comida. L E   O S E R E M

_____ 2. Es el dinero que das por el buen servicio. A L   R O N P I P A

_____ 3. Es el acto de llevarle la comida al cliente. E R T A R

_____ 4. Es algo dulce que pides en un restaurante. L E   T E P R O S

_____ 5. Es la mujer que trae la comida. A L   M A R E S E

_____ 6. Es el acto de decirle al mesero qué quieres. I P R E D

*G*ramática   The preterite of **pedir** and **servir**   *Pupil's Edition, p. 154*

Pedir *(to ask for)* and **servir** *(to serve)* have stem changes in the third-person singular and plural forms of the preterite: **pidió, pidieron; sirvió, sirvieron.**

15 Alice wrote you a note about the disastrous lunch she had with some friends. Complete her description with the correct preterite forms of the verbs.

Fui al Restaurante Fuentes ayer con unos compañeros. Yo

(1) _____ (pedir) ensalada de frutas y pan ¡pero el

mesero me **(2)** _____ (servir) sopa de pollo! Maida y

Jacco **(3)** _____ (pedir) perros calientes y refrescos.

Pero, ¿sabes qué? Los meseros les **(4)** _____ (servir)

ensalada de frutas. Luego la mesera no nos **(5)** _____

(servir) el flan que nosotros **(6)** _____ (pedir). Cuando

Claudia le **(7)** _____ (pedir) el flan otra vez, la mesera

respondió, "Nosotros **(8)** _____ (servir) todo el flan

ayer. No hay más". Le preguntamos, "¿Ustedes ya **(9)** _____

(servir) todo el flan?" Luego nos fuimos, y claro que no dejamos

una propina.

Nota Gramatical   The preterite of **traer**   *Pupil's Edition, p. 154*

The preterite of **traer** is: **traje, trajiste, trajo, trajimos,** trajisteis, **trajeron.**

16 Erika is talking about what she and her friends brought to the booster club party. Complete her description with the correct preterite forms of **traer.**

1. Yo _____ sándwiches de queso.

2. Hernán y yo _____ papitas pero nadie las comió.

3. Vicente y Khalid _____ una ensalada.

4. Y para tomar, Rhonda _____ limonada y té frío.

5. Y tú, ¿qué _____?

17 Caleb is reporting to his Spanish class about his evening out with his friends. Complete his description by writing the correct preterite form of each verb in parentheses.

```
Bueno, yo (1) _____ (pedir) el arroz con pollo. Erin y

Jake (2) _____ (pedir) la sopa de legumbres y Ben

(3) _____ (pedir) un sándwich de jamón y queso. Un

mesero y una mesera nos (4) _____ (traer) la comida. Luego

nosotros (5) _____ (pedir) pastel de chocolate. Pero el

mesero se olvidó de traerle el pastel a Erin. El mesero le preguntó,

"¿Yo no le (6) _____ (traer) el postre, señorita?" Por

fin el mesero le (7) _____ (servir) el postre. Por último

pagamos la cuenta, dejamos la propina y nos fuimos.
```

18 What happened the last time you went out to eat with your relatives or friends?

1. ¿Qué pediste?

_____

2. ¿Qué pidieron tus parientes *(relatives)* o amigos/as?

_____

3. ¿Quién trajo la comida?

_____

4. ¿Trajeron todas las cosas que pediste?

_____

CAPÍTULO 6 Tercer Paso

¿Te acuerdas? How food tastes *Pupil's Edition, p. 155*

19 Write the word or phrase you associate with the things/foods listed.

1. el gazpacho, el hielo, el helado _____

2. un plato delicioso _____

3. las galletas, el pastel, el chocolate _____

4. los chiles, el ají _____

20 Dawana is commenting on her food while she has lunch with Brandon. Write the questions she asked him, using **estar** and the correct forms of adjectives from the word bank.

caliente	dulce	frío	picante	rico	salado

DAWANA (1) ¿_____?

BRANDON Sí, la sopa tiene mucha sal.

DAWANA (2) ¿_____?

BRANDON Sí, la ensalada está deliciosa. Me gusta mucho.

DAWANA (3) ¿_____?

BRANDON Sí, mi bistec está como hielo.

DAWANA (4) ¿_____?

BRANDON Sí. Creo que el helado tiene mucho azúcar.

DAWANA (5) ¿_____?

BRANDON Para mí, no. La salsa no tiene mucho chile.

21 Write one or two sentences about each topic to describe the last time you went out to eat. Be sure to answer the following questions:

1. Who went with you?
2. What did each person order?
3. Who served you, and did this person bring you what you ordered?
4. Did you leave a tip? Why or why not?

1. _____

2. _____

3. _____

4. _____

Grammar and Vocabulary Workbook, Teacher's Edition **53**

CAPÍTULO 6 Tercer Paso

Nombre _____ Clase _____ Fecha _____

7 ¿Conoces bien tu pasado?

■ PRIMER PASO

To talk about what you used to do, as well as what you used to like and dislike, you'll need to use the imperfect tense.

*G*ramática   The imperfect tense   *Pupil's Edition, p. 172*

To talk about what you used to do or what you were like in the past, use the imperfect tense.

Yo **hacía** la tarea todos los días.

Mis hermanas siempre **sacaban** mejores notas.

1 Write the indicated forms of these verbs in the imperfect.

1. hablar (yo) _____

2. comer (ellos) _____

3. escribir (nosotros) _____

4. poner (tú) _____

5. dar (Marta y yo) _____

6. comprar (Juan y Ana) _____

7. beber (usted) _____

8. salir (tú) _____

9. vivir (ustedes) _____

10. estudiar (Juan) _____

2 Roberto is telling Carla about his life when he was younger. Complete his sentences with the correct imperfect forms of the verbs in parentheses.

Cuando yo (1) _____ (tener) diez años

(2) _____ (estar) muy contento. Mi familia

(3) _____ (vivir) en San Juan. Todos los

días mis amigos y yo (4) _____ (jugar) en

la playa. Mi hermano (5) _____ (nadar)

y mis hermanas (6) _____ (correr) por la

playa. Carla, (7) ¿ _____ (pasar) tú mucho

tiempo en la playa?

3 Find out what the following famous people used to do when they were young by combining elements from the three columns. Be sure to use the imperfect tense.

COLUMN A	COLUMN B	COLUMN C
El escritor Carlos Fuentes	hacer	a la gente de su pueblo
La cantante Linda Ronstadt	escribir	mucho ejercicio
El artista Pablo Picasso	pintar	muchas cartas
La tenista Arantxa Sánchez Vicario	cantar	canciones para su padre
El jugador de fútbol americano Dan Marino	practicar	el tenis todos los días

1. _____

2. _____

3. _____

4. _____

5. _____

4 Paula is talking on the phone to her pen pal. Write the questions that her pen pal asked her.

GLORIA (1) ¿_____?

PAULA Vivía en Guatemala cuando era niña.

GLORIA (2) ¿_____?

PAULA Mi familia y yo pasábamos los veranos en Antigua.

GLORIA (3) ¿_____?

PAULA En el verano jugaba mucho al fútbol con mis amigos allá en Antigua.

GLORIA (4) ¿_____?

PAULA No hacía ni mucho calor ni mucho frío.

GLORIA (5) ¿_____?

PAULA Normalmente regresaba a casa a las siete porque cenábamos temprano.

5 You're being interviewed for your school newspaper. Answer the following questions about what life was like when you were nine years old.

1. ¿A qué escuela asistías?

   _____

2. ¿Con quién almorzabas en la cafetería?

   _____

3. ¿Cómo se llamaban tus maestros entonces?

   _____

4. ¿Tenías muchos amigos?

   _____

5. ¿Qué hacías por la tarde después de tus clases?

   _____

Grammar and Vocabulary Workbook, Teacher's Edition **55**

Nota Gramatical The imperfect of **ir** and **ver** *Pupil's Edition, p. 173*

The verbs **ir** and **ver** are irregular in the imperfect tense.

IR		VER	
iba	íbamos	veía	veíamos
ibas	ibais	veías	veíais
iba	iban	veía	veían

6 Cristina is telling her Spanish teacher what she and her family used to see when they went to various places. Complete Cristina's sentences with the imperfect forms of **ir** or **ver**.

1. Cuando Raúl y Julio _____ al colegio, _____ a todos sus amigos.

2. Cuando Jennifer _____ al parque, _____ muchas flores.

3. Cuando nosotros _____ al cine, _____ películas cómicas.

4. Cuando yo _____ al museo, _____ arte moderno.

5. Y usted, señor, cuando era niño, ¿adónde _____ y qué _____?

VOCABULARIO   Childhood activities   *Pupil's Edition, p. 174*

7 Complete the crossword puzzle using the clues provided.

Horizontales

1. A Diego le gustaba _____ casas de cartas.

5. David no era muy simpático; le gustaba _____ con los otros chicos.

6. María siempre hacía _____. Un día asustó a su hermano menor y lo hizo llorar.

7. A Patricio no le gustaba _____ sus juguetes con otros niños.

Verticales

1. Carla es una persona cómica. Siempre cuenta _____ en clase.

2. De niña a Patricia le gustaba _____ a los árboles con sus hermanos.

3. En clase Pablo no trabajaba. Prefería _____ ____ ser un actor famoso.

4. Si Pablo ve una araña *(spider)*, va a _____ .

■ SEGUNDO PASO

To describe what people and things were like, you may need to use conjunctions, the verbs **ser** and **haber** in the imperfect tense, and some appropriate adjectives. You may also want to talk about city life and public services.

> Nota *Gramatical*   When to change **y** to **e** and **o** to **u**   *Pupil's Edition, p. 177*
>
> The conjunction **y** *(and)* changes to **e** before a word beginning with an "i" sound.
> The conjunction **o** *(or)* changes to **u** before a word beginning with an "o" sound.
>   Pablo **e** Hilaria van a venir mañana.
>   ¿Hay más mujeres **u** hombres en tu clase?

8 Alejandro is describing some of his friends. Fill in the blanks with **y** or **e**, as appropriate.

1. Clemente es divertido _____ inteligente. Es un estudiante muy aplicado.

2. Marta y Luisa son listas _____ cómicas y cuentan muchos chistes.

3. Carolina es tímida _____ introvertida. No habla mucho en clase.

4. Pilar y Jasón son altos _____ atléticos y practican muchos deportes.

5. José es un poco rebelde _____ irresponsable pero es una persona buena.

6. Pamela y Carmen son bonitas _____ elegantes y son inteligentes también.

7. Diana es misteriosa _____ interesante y me gusta hablar con ella.

8. Héctor _____ Ignacio son buenos amigos. Practican el fútbol juntos.

9 Laura is asking her family about their plans for their summer trip to Florida. Complete her questions with **o** or **u**.

1. ¿Vamos a estar en la playa por siete _____ ocho días, mamá?

2. ¿Vamos a Miami _____ a Orlando? ¿Y cuál vamos a visitar primero?

3. ¿Compramos billetes para dos días en Disney World _____ uno, papá?

4. ¿Es bonito _____ ordinario el Hotel Reina de la Playa?

5. ¿Está en la calle noventa _____ ochenta nuestro hotel?

6. ¿Vamos a bucear _____ nadar el fin de semana que viene?

7. ¿Tenemos diez _____ once días de vacaciones este verano?

8. ¿Salimos a las nueve _____ a las ocho el sábado?

9. ¿Cuál de mis primos va a venir, Lucinda _____ Honorato?

10. ¿Reservamos nuestros boletos para el avión mañana _____ hoy?

Nota Gramatical The imperfect of ser *Pupil's Edition, p. 179*

The forms of **ser** in the imperfect are:

yo **era**	nosotros **éramos**
tú **eras**	vosotros erais
él / ella / usted **era**	ellos / ellas / ustedes **eran**

10 Luis is talking to his friend Gina about how things have changed since they graduated from high school ten years ago. Fill in the blanks with the correct imperfect forms of the verb **ser**.

Gina, en el colegio tú (**1**) _____ muy conservadora pero ahora eres

liberal. Oye, mira. Allí está Julia. Antes ella (**2**) _____ rubia pero

ahora es morena. Allí a la derecha están Josefina y su hermana. Ellas

(**3**) _____ bajas pero ahora son altas. Siempre quería hablar con

ellas pero antes yo (**4**) _____ muy tímido. Ahora soy mucho más

extrovertido. Nosotros (**5**) _____ muy jóvenes, ¿no? ¡Pero ahora todos

somos tan viejos!

11 Write sentences telling an old friend what the following people were like as children. Be sure to use the imperfect tense. Your sentences may be affirmative or negative.

> creativo inteligente divertido travieso
>
> extrovertido tímido simpático cómico

1. Mis padres _____

   _____ .

2. Mi mejor amigo/a _____

   _____ .

3. Mi profesor/a _____

   _____ .

4. Mi abuelo/a _____

   _____ .

5. Yo _____

   _____ .

6. Tú y yo _____

   _____ .

¡Ven conmigo! Level 2, Chapter 7

VOCABULARIO   Describing people   *Pupil's Edition, p. 178*

12 Read the following descriptions of Gerardo's childhood friends. Write **sí** beside the descriptions if they make sense and **no** if they don't. If a description isn't logical, make it logical by rewriting the second sentence of the description in the space provided.

_____ 1. Enrique era consentido. Siempre recibía todo lo que pedía.

_____

_____ 2. Susana era muy conversadora. No le gustaba hablar con nadie.

_____

_____ 3. Marco era un chico bondadoso. Nunca ayudaba a los otros estudiantes con sus problemas.

_____

_____ 4. Lupita era bastante impaciente. Ella nunca podía esperar sin quejarse.

_____

_____ 5. Humberto era solitario. Prefería estar con mucha gente.

_____

13 Read about what the following people used to do when they were younger. Then, use an adjective from the word bank to write a sentence about each person.

impaciente	bondadoso	egoísta	aventurero	solitario	conversador

MODELO   Tú pasabas todo el día hablando por teléfono.
Tú eras muy conversador.

1. Claudia pasaba horas y horas sola en la playa.

_____

2. Mis dos hermanos escalaban montañas, buceaban y viajaban a muchos lugares exóticos.

_____

3. Mi madre era voluntaria en el hospital.

_____

4. Yo nunca hacía cola porque no me gustaba esperar.

_____

5. Hernán nunca compartía dulces con sus hermanos.

_____

6. Tú hablabas todo el tiempo con tus amigos.

_____

Grammar and Vocabulary Workbook, Teacher's Edition **59**

VOCABULARIO   City life   *Pupil's Edition, p. 180*

14 Write the vocabulary words that have the **opposite** meaning of the words below. Then circle the opposite words in the puzzle.

1. silencio _____

2. aire puro _____

3. pequeño _____

4. tranquilo _____

5. difícil _____

```
N  Ó  I  C  A  N  I  M  A  T  N  O  C
A  S  Q  W  E  N  D  L  R  P  I  B  Z
G  I  G  A  N  T  E  S  C  O  Z  M  U
O  V  F  E  M  A  O  M  Q  R  E  A  O
Ó  N  C  I  O  D  R  U  I  D  O  S  O
A  F  E  R  I  C  O  N  T  M  I  S  R
T  V  B  U  X  A  E  U  I  O  S  O  D
E  O  R  Y  Z  O  L  L  I  C  N  E  S
```

15 Complete this paragraph with the correct forms of the words in the word bank.

> ruido   fábrica   gigantesco   tránsito
> sencillo   aire puro   contaminación

En aquellos días Miami era mucho más pequeño. Los edificios no eran

(1) _____ como ahora. El (2) _____ no era un

problema porque no había carros. La música era más bonita. Ahora lo que los jóvenes

llaman música es, en mi opinión, puro (3) _____. El agua y las

playas eran más limpias porque no había (4) _____ de las

(5) _____. Ah, la vida era mucho más (6) _____.

VOCABULARIO   Public services and conveniences   *Pupil's Edition, p. 181*

16 Which of the things in the word bank would you use in the following situations?

> la estufa   el aire acondicionado   la calefacción
> la lámpara de la calle   el agua corriente

_____ 1. Hace mucho frío en la casa.

_____ 2. Tienes sed y quieres un vaso de agua.

_____ 3. Hace mucho calor en la casa.

_____ 4. Vas a preparar una cena especial para tus padres.

Nota Gramatical   The imperfect of hay   *Pupil's Edition, p. 180*

Remember that **hay** means *there are* or *there is*. The imperfect of **hay** is **había**, which means *there was*, *there were*, or *there used to be*. The plural forms are the same as the singular.

17 Mr. Arce is telling his class what his city was like when he was a teenager. Complete his description by rearranging the words below and using the imperfect of **hay**.

1. mi ciudad / en / menos / hay / violencia

   _____

2. más / parques / hay / los / en / árboles

   _____

3. hay / playas / en / menos / hoteles / las

   _____

4. las / tránsito / ciudades / menos / en / hay

   _____

5. del / contaminación / menos / aire / hay / también

   _____

18 Find out what life was like in Ponce according to Uncle Martín by filling in the blanks with **había** or the correct imperfect form of **ser.**

Cuando (1) _____ niño la vida (2) _____ mucho

más tranquila. No (3) _____ tanta contaminación de los carros. El aire

(4) _____ puro y el agua, clara. No (5) _____

peligro *(danger)* en las ciudades como ahora. Caminaba solo por la noche sin

preocuparme. Mi familia platicaba por la noche. (6) _____ unas

conversaciones muy interesantes. Ahora todos miran la televisión. Ah, la vida en aquellos

días (7) _____ bellísima.

19 What were the following people and things like ten years ago? Complete the sentences using the imperfect tense.

1. Mi escuela _____

   _____ .

2. La calle donde yo vivía _____

   _____ .

3. Mis amigos/as _____

   _____ .

■ TERCER PASO

To describe people, you may want to use comparisons of equality.

> *G*ramática   Comparisons of equality   *Pupil's Edition, p. 183*
>
> Use **tan** + *adjective* or *adverb* + **como** to compare qualities of people or things that are the same or equal.
>
> Yo soy **tan** responsable **como** Michael.
> Él llegó a clase **tan** tarde **como** yo.
> Juan corre **tan** rápidamente **como** Ana.

20 Claudia is comparing her dogs Jazz and Pablo. The only difference between them is that Jazz is larger and runs faster. Write what Claudia says, using comparisons of equality.

MODELO   simpático   **Pablo es tan simpático como Jazz.**

1. independiente _____

2. fuerte _____

3. bonito _____

4. rebelde _____

5. inteligente _____

6. impaciente _____

21 Read the following descriptions. Then use the adjectives and adverbs in the word bank to compare the players on Raúl's football team.

grande	alto	inteligente	fuerte	rápido	tarde

1. Gilberto puede levantar 90 kilos. Rafael también puede levantar 90 kilos.

_____

2. Alejo mide 3 metros y Andrés mide 3 metros también.

_____

3. El partido empezó a las dos. Ricardo llegó a las dos y cuarto y Paco también.

_____

4. Emilio y Sergio corrieron cien metros en once segundos hoy.

_____

5. Gustavo y Francisco pesan *(weigh)* 250 libras.

_____

¡Ven conmigo! Level 2, Chapter 7

> ### *G*ramática   Comparisons of equality   *Pupil's Edition, p. 183*
>
> To compare quantities that are the same or equal, use the following formulas:
>
> **tanto / tantos** + *noun* + **como**
>
> **tanta / tantas** + *noun* + **como**
>
> Hay **tanto** tránsito en Miami **como** en Nueva York.
>
> Había **tantas** chicas **como** chicos en mi clase.

22 Gloria is comparing her classes with her sister's classes. Complete her sentences with **tanto**, **tantos**, **tanta**, or **tantas**.

1. Yo tengo _____ clases como tú, Margarita.

2. Mis profesores no dan _____ tarea como tus profesores.

3. Necesito leer _____ libros para mi clase de literatura como tú.

4. No tengo _____ problemas en matemáticas como tú.

5. En mis clases los estudiantes no hacen _____ ruido como en tus clases.

6. No hay _____ estudiantes en mis clases como en tus clases.

23 Marta works weekends in a supermarket. Write comparisons of equality based on her inventory list.

MODELO   24 naranjas; 24 manzanas

         Hay tantas naranjas como manzanas.

1. *39 plátanos; 39 piñas*

    _____

2. *123 refrescos de naranja; 123 refrescos de limón*

    _____

3. *75 naranjas; 75 piñas*

    _____

4. *40 litros de leche; 40 litros de jugo de naranja*

    _____

5. *50 kilos de carne de res; 50 kilos de pollo*

    _____

CAPÍTULO

8 Diversiones

■ PRIMER PASO

To describe a past event, you may want to use -**ísimo/a** endings to express *really* or *extremely,* as well as superlatives (*the most* . . . , *the least* . . . , etc.). You may also want to talk about places you've been, such as movies, amusement parks, and zoos.

> Nota *G*ramatical   Adjectives ending in **ísimo/a**   *Pupil's Edition, p. 197*
>
> In English, we emphasize adjectives by placing *really* or *extremely* in front of them. To emphasize an adjective in Spanish, drop the vowel ending of the adjective and add -**ísimo, -ísimos, -ísima,** or -**ísimas**.
>
> La vida en París era cara pero en Nueva York era **carísima**.

1 Rafael is very proud of his brother. Complete the following paragraph by adding the -**ísimo/a** endings to the adjectives and adverbs in parentheses.

Mi hermano mayor Esteban es **(1)** _____ (inteligente). Saca

notas **(2)** _____ (bueno) en todas sus clases. Toma

unas clases **(3)** _____ (difícil). También juega al fútbol con

sus amigos. Esteban y sus amigos son **(4)** _____

(alto) y **(5)** _____ (rápido). Esteban

tiene una novia **(6)** _____ (guapo). Ella también

es **(7)** _____ (interesante). Yo quiero ser exactamente como mi

hermano Esteban.

2 Use the adjectives below to write sentences describing people or things you're familiar with. Use the -**ísimo/a** ending.

1. (divertido) _____

2. (difícil) _____

3. (contento) _____

4. (importante) _____

5. (ocupado) _____

6. (alto) _____

VOCABULARIO   Places of recreation   *Pupil's Edition, p. 198*

3 Cecilia went to a lot of places this weekend. Indicate whether she saw the following things at the **a) zoológico**, **b) parque de atracciones**, or **c) cine**.

_____ 1. un cocodrilo de Florida   _____ 5. una estrella de Hollywood

_____ 2. el estreno de *Justicia*   _____ 6. un loro de muchos colores

_____ 3. una serpiente   _____ 7. unos carros chocones

_____ 4. una montaña rusa grande   _____ 8. una rueda de Chicago gigantesca

4 Sergio went to the zoo this weekend. Write the names of the animals he saw.

_____ 1. Este animal peligroso pasa mucho tiempo en el agua y tiene una boca grande con muchos dientes.

_____ 2. A este animal le gusta trepar a los árboles y comer plátanos.

_____ 3. Este pájaro *(bird)* es de muchos colores.

_____ 4. Este animal tranquilo nada en el agua y camina despacio.

_____ 5. Este animal es delgado y largo y puede ser peligroso.

*G*ramática   Superlatives   *Pupil's Edition, p. 199*

1. To refer to people or things as *the most* or *the least*, use the following formula:
   definite article + *noun* + **más** / **menos** + *adjective* (+ **de**)
   El actor más guapo de España es Antonio Banderas.

5 Unscramble the following sentences to find out what the famous movie critic Jaime Miratodo had to say about the **Festival de Cine Ponceño**.

1. más / es la estrella / Lupita Cárdenas / de Hollywood / bella

_____

_____

2. del festival / tiene los efectos especiales / *Galaxias VI* / maravillosos / más

_____

_____

3. *Silvio* / del festival / menos / fue el estreno / popular

_____

_____

4. Felipe Sooner / original / más / de hoy / es el director

_____

_____

6 Imagine you're a contestant on a TV game show. Use clues from each word box to write appropriate questions for the following answers. Be sure to use **¿Cuál es . . . ?**.

animal   país
serpiente
deporte   perra

grande   pequeño
largo
famoso   popular

África   mundo
América Latina
Hollywood   Puerto Rico

1. La respuesta es *El Salvador.*

   ¿ _____ ?

2. La respuesta es *el elefante.*

   ¿ _____ ?

3. La respuesta es *Lassie®.*

   ¿ _____ ?

4. La respuesta es *la pitón.*

   ¿ _____ ?

5. La respuesta es *el béisbol.*

   ¿ _____ ?

Gramática   The superlatives **mejor** and **peor**   *Pupil's Edition, p. 199*

2. **Bueno** and **malo** have the irregular forms **mejor** and **peor**. Notice that you don't need to use **más** or **menos**.

En mi opinión, la **mejor** actriz del mundo es Glenn Close.

La **peor** película del festival fue *Andrés.*

---

7 Patricia has very strong opinions about three amusement parks. Complete her descriptions with the appropriate superlatives.

MODELO   Los perros calientes en Dallas y Houston son buenos pero los perros calientes en Atlanta son **los mejores del mundo.**

1. Las montañas rusas en Houston y Dallas son malas pero la montaña rusa en Atlanta es

   _____ .

2. Los carros chocones en Dallas y Atlanta son buenos pero los carros chocones en Houston

   son _____ .

3. Las ruedas de Chicago en Dallas y Atlanta son malas pero la rueda de Chicago en Houston

   es _____ .

4. Las hamburguesas en Atlanta y Houston son buenas pero las hamburguesas en Dallas son

   _____ .

■ SEGUNDO PASO

To say why you couldn't do something, you may want to refer to running errands. You may also need to use verbs followed by prepositions as well as talk about things that were going on at the same time.

VOCABULARIO   Running errands   *Pupil's Edition, p. 201*

8 Emilio ran some errands for his father yesterday. Put the list of places that he went in the correct order from 1 to 6 according to the following chart.

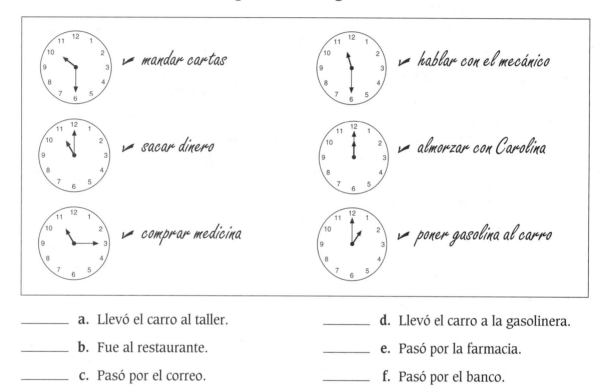

_____ **a.** Llevó el carro al taller.

_____ **b.** Fue al restaurante.

_____ **c.** Pasó por el correo.

_____ **d.** Llevó el carro a la gasolinera.

_____ **e.** Pasó por la farmacia.

_____ **f.** Pasó por el banco.

9 Based on what the following people said to Mrs. Garza, describe the errands she was running.

MODELO   —Debe lavarse los dientes todos los días. **Ella fue a una cita con el dentista.**

1. —Señora, es necesario cambiar el motor de su carro.

_____

2. —Usted necesita tomar la medicina cada dos horas y llamar al doctor mañana.

_____

3. —¿Debo llenar el tanque, señora?

_____

4. —Aquí tiene sus cheques de viajero.

_____

5. —Sí, señora, necesita dos estampillas de cincuenta centavos.

_____

Nota Gramatical   Verbs followed by a preposition   *Pupil's Edition, p. 203*

Many of the verbs you've already learned are followed by a preposition.
Julio se bajaba **del** autobús mientras Macarena se subía **al** autobús.

10 Find out about Cristóbal's dream by combining the elements in the first column with the elements in the second column. Write the completed sentences in the blanks below.

COLUMN A	COLUMN B
1. Anoche yo soñé. . .	de que hablé con Mike Shanahan.
2. Me acuerdo. . .	a mi primer partido profesional.
3. Me dijo que era necesario aumentar. . .	con ser jugador profesional de fútbol americano.
4. El siguiente *(next)* domingo asistí. . .	en jugar otra vez el lunes por la noche.
5. Después del partido Troy Aikman y yo quedamos. . .	de peso para jugar bien.

1. _____

_____

2. _____

_____

3. _____

_____

4. _____

_____

5. _____

_____

11 Inés is writing a letter to her friend Héctor to tell him about what happened to her today. Fill in the blanks with the correct prepositions.

Nunca vas a creer lo que me pasó hoy. Yo hablé (**1**) _____

teléfono con María y me dijo que este fin de semana fue

(**2**) _____ San Antonio. Tenía que reunirse

(**3**) _____ su padre. Ellos pasaban (**4**) _____

el Paseo del Río cuando vieron a Juan, mi novio. Montaba

(**5**) _____ bicicleta con mi mejor amiga Jennifer. ¿Qué

debo hacer?

Nota *G*ramatical   The imperfect with **mientras**   *Pupil's Edition, p. 204*

To talk about two things that were happening at the same time in the past, use **mientras** and the imperfect tense.

Ellos **miraban** la televisión **mientras** José **estudiaba**.

12 Lina is talking to you about what was going on at the gym last night. Fill in the blanks with the imperfect tense of the verbs in parentheses to find out what everyone was doing.

Había mucha gente en el Gimnasio Benavides el sábado por la noche. A las cinco Julio

jugaba al baloncesto. Él **(1)** _____ (jugar) mientras su amigo

Emiliano y yo **(2)** _____ (hablar) con Josefina. A las cinco y cuarto

Carolina empezó a levantar pesas. Ella **(3)** _____ (levantar) pesas

mientras Susana y Juan **(4)** _____ (asistir) a una clase de aeróbicos.

A las cinco y media Toby practicaba el atletismo. Él **(5)** _____

(correr) mientras tú **(6)** _____ (estirarse), ¿no?

13 Based on the clues, tell what Katrina and Vladimir were doing at each time of day.

MODELO   A las ocho y media Katrina estaba en el Cine Mar y Vladimir estaba en su oficina.
Katrina miraba una película mientras Vladimir trabajaba.

estudiar   poner   acompañar   mandar

correr   comprar   comer   sacar

1. A las cuatro y media Katrina estaba en el correo y Vladimir estaba en el banco.

   _____

   _____

2. A las cinco y cuarto Vladimir estaba en la biblioteca y Katrina estaba en el Supermercado Muchacomida.

   _____

   _____

3. A las seis Vladimir estaba en el Restaurante Fruto del Mar y Katrina estaba en la gasolinera Petro-Stop.

   _____

   _____

CAPÍTULO 8 Segundo paso

■ TERCER PASO

To report what someone said, you'll need to use the verb **decir** in the preterite. You may also want to use festival vocabulary to tell people about fun things others did.

VOCABULARIO   Festivals   *Pupil's Edition, p. 207*

14 Unscramble the following words, using the clues given. Then, use the letters in the highlighted squares to write another word for **disfrutar**.

1. Gente, músicos y carrozas pasan por la calle. **siledef**

   [⊙][⊙][ ][⊙][ ][ ]

2. Es un traje de Halloween. **zrfaids**

   [ ][⊙][ ][ ][ ][ ][ ]

3. Es el acto de poner decoraciones. **roecrda**

   [ ][ ][ ][ ][ ][⊙][ ]

4. Es una gran fiesta... por ejemplo, para celebrar un día nacional. **stveilfa**

   [ ][⊙][ ][⊙][ ][⊙][ ][ ]

5. Son carros grandes con decoraciones. **caorrzsa**

   [ ][ ][⊙][ ][ ][ ][⊙][ ]

   En los festivales, a la gente le gusta _____.

15 Now use the words you unscrambled in activity 14 to fill in Karin's e-mail to Wendy about her trip to Puerto Rico.

Este fin de semana fui a Hatillo, un pequeño pueblo aquí en Puerto

Rico. Asistí al (**1**) _____ de Las Máscaras. Había un

(**2**) _____ enorme con músicos que pasaba por las calles.

Un grupo de estudiantes diseñó una (**3**) _____ muy bonita.

Era un carro decorado con flores de Puerto Rico. Ellos empezaron a

(**4**) _____ el carro en octubre. Un hombre tenía un

(**5**) _____ increíble de pantalones, chaqueta, sombrero y

máscara amarillos. Fue maravilloso.

   Un abrazo bien fuerte de tu amiga,

   Karin

---

*G*ramática   The preterite of **decir**   *Pupil's Edition, p. 208*

1. The verb **decir** *(to tell)* is irregular in the preterite.

yo **dije**	nosotros **dijimos**
tú **dijiste**	vosotros dijisteis
él / ella / usted **dijo**	ellos / ellas / ustedes **dijeron**

2. When reporting how someone felt in the past, use **decir** in the preterite followed by the imperfect of a verb that expresses emotions or reactions.

   Pablo me **dijo** que no le **gustaba** la fiesta.

   Yo le **dije** a Ricardo que **estaba** enojado.

16 Sandra is upset because she thinks Rolando has been gossiping about her. Fill in the blanks in their conversation with the correct preterite forms of **decir**.

SANDRA   ¿Por qué (1) _____ tú que yo no soy buena estudiante?

ROLANDO   Te digo la pura verdad, Sandra, yo no lo (2) _____.

SANDRA   Entonces ¿quién lo (3) _____? La verdad es que creo que lo

   (4) _____ tú y Raquel.

ROLANDO   ¡Ay no, Sandra! Raquel y yo no lo (5) _____. ¡Yo creo que lo

   (6) _____ Mónica!

SANDRA   No, ya hablé con ella y ella no lo (7) _____.

ROLANDO   ¡Entonces lo (8) _____ Berta y José! ¡Habla con ellos!

17 Carlos is talking about what people told him about the party last night. Write what he says according to the model.

MODELO   Carlos y Juan / hay mucha gente

   Carlos y Juan me dijeron que había mucha gente.

1. Anita / la música ser muy buena

   _____

2. Miguel y Carmen / todos estar muy contentos

   _____

3. Susana / ella estar muy cansada después de la fiesta

   _____

4. Tú / la comida estar deliciosa

   _____

5. Y Sofía / a ella no gustarle la música

   _____

⁹ ¡Día de mercado!

CAPÍTULO

■ PRIMER PASO

To ask for and give directions, you'll need to use formal commands as well as some specific vocabulary related to getting around town.

VOCABULARIO   Getting around town   *Pupil's Edition, p. 226*

1 Based on the directions below, write the letter corresponding to each place on the map.

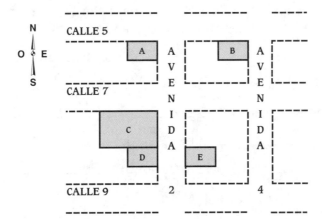

_____ 1. La Joyería Cristóbal está en la esquina de la Calle 5 y la Avenida 4.

_____ 2. El Cine Mar está a una cuadra al oeste de la Joyería Cristóbal.

_____ 3. El Restaurante Rancho Luna está en la esquina de la Calle 7 y la Avenida 2.

_____ 4. La Zapatería Tica Linda está al lado del Restaurante Rancho Luna.

_____ 5. El Supermercado Más por Menos está delante de la Zapatería Tica Linda.

2 Now use the map in Activity 1 to give directions to the following places.

1. Estoy en "**B**" y necesito ir a "**E**".

_____

_____

2. Estoy en "**C**" y necesito ir a "**B**".

_____

_____

3. Estoy en "**A**" y necesito ir a la esquina de la Calle 9 y la Avenida 4.

_____

_____

CAPÍTULO 9 Primer paso

*G*ramática   Formal commands   *Pupil's Edition, p. 228*

1. Formal commands are used with people you address as **usted** and **ustedes**. Here's how to form these commands:
Using the present-tense **yo** form, drop the **-o** ending, and...
   a. for **-ar** verbs add **-e** or **-en**:
   Estudi<u>o</u> → ¡Estudi<u>e</u> (usted)!   ¡Estudi<u>en</u> (ustedes)!
   b. for **-er** and **-ir** verbs add **-a** or **-an**:
   Com<u>o</u> → ¡Com<u>a</u> (usted)!   ¡Com<u>an</u> (ustedes)!
   Viv<u>o</u> → ¡Viv<u>a</u> (usted)!   ¡Viv<u>an</u> (ustedes)!

3 You're taking your neighbor's children to the circus. Tell them what to do and not to do, using **ustedes** commands.

MODELO   ¡**No caminen** (caminar) rápidamente!

1. _____ (beber) agua antes de salir.
2. _____ (cerrar) las ventanas antes de salir.
3. _____ (abrir) la puerta del carro.
4. _____ (escribir) en los boletos.
5. _____ (comer) demasiado.
6. _____ (esperar) pacientemente.

4 Using formal commands, tell the following people what to do to solve their problems.

visitar	descansar	preparar	leer	abrir	estudiar

1. Tu abuela está muy cansada porque no durmió muy bien anoche.

_____

2. Roberto y Catalina tienen un examen mañana y están preocupados.

_____

3. Hace calor y no hay aire acondicionado en el carro del señor Obregón.

_____

4. Los García quieren saber más sobre la historia del arte moderno.

_____

5. La señora Maldonado no sabe qué debe preparar para la cena.

_____

6. La profesora Hernández quiere saber más sobre el béisbol.

_____

Grammar and Vocabulary Workbook, Teacher's Edition **73**

CAPÍTULO 9 Primer paso

*G*ramática   More formal commands   *Pupil's Edition, p. 228*

2. Stem-changing verbs and verbs with irregular **yo** forms in the present indicative have the same changes in **usted** and **ustedes** commands.

Cierro →	**¡Cierre** (usted)!	**¡Cierren** (ustedes)!
Tengo →	**¡Tenga** (usted)!	**¡Tengan** (ustedes)!

3. Verbs ending in **-car**, **-gar**, and **-zar** have the following spelling changes.

buscar	(c → qu)	Bus**co**	**¡Busque** (usted)!	**¡Busquen** (ustedes)!
jugar	(g → gu)	Jue**go**	**¡Juegue** (usted)!	**¡Jueguen** (ustedes)!
empezar	(z → c)	Empie**zo**	**¡Empiece** (usted)!	**¡Empiecen** (ustedes)!

4. These five verbs have irregular formal commands:

dar	→	**dé, den**	saber →	**sepa, sepan**	ir →	**vaya, vayan**
estar	→	**esté, estén**	ser →	**sea, sean**		

5 Imagine that you're working for the the Bureau of Tourism in San Antonio. Help the tourists that have called you by filling in the blanks with the correct formal commands.

Sí, señor. Primero **(1)** _____ (ir) usted a la calle Commerce.

(2) _____ (Seguir) todo derecho hasta la calle Álamo.

(3) _____ (Buscar) un lugar en el estacionamiento al lado de la pastelería.

¿Ustedes tienen ocho personas en el grupo? **(4)** _____ (Ir) al Restaurante

Mexipollo. Es muy grande. **(5)** _____ (Pedir) una mesa en el patio porque

es muy bonito. No **(6)** _____ (llegar) tarde porque cierran a las nueve.

6 Imagine you're a counselor at a nature camp in Miami. Use negative **ustedes** commands to answer your campers' questions.

1. ¿Podemos jugar con la serpiente?

   _____

2. ¿Podemos despertar al cocodrilo?

   _____

3. ¿Podemos darle nuestras hamburguesas a la tortuga?

   _____

4. ¿Podemos pescar aquí?

   _____

5. ¿Podemos tocar estas plantas?

   _____

*G*ramática   Reflexive pronouns with commands   *Pupil's Edition, p. 228*

5. Reflexive pronouns come before negative commands and are attached to affirmative commands.

No **se laven** las manos allí.   **Lávense** las manos en el baño.

7 Rosemary is babysitting her twin brothers Basil and Tim. Complete the following sentences with plural formal commands.

1. No _____ ustedes en la mesa. (sentarse)

2. No _____ en la piscina. (bañarse)

3. _____ el pelo con el champú. (Lavarse)

4. _____ los dientes después de comer. (Cepillarse)

5. No _____ la cara. (afeitarse)

6. No _____ la ropa de su papá. (ponerse)

7. _____ ahora mismo. (Acostarse)

8 Write advertising slogans by combining elements from each column. Be sure to use **usted** commands.

1. ¡Despertarse | con las toallas Suavecitas!
2. ¡No vestirse | si no se va a poner los bluejeans de Vaquero!
3. ¡Secarse | el pelo con champú ordinario! ¡Use Lavabella!
4. ¡No lavarse | a tiempo con los despertadores Cascabel!
5. ¡Bañarse | con nuestro jabón Esencia!

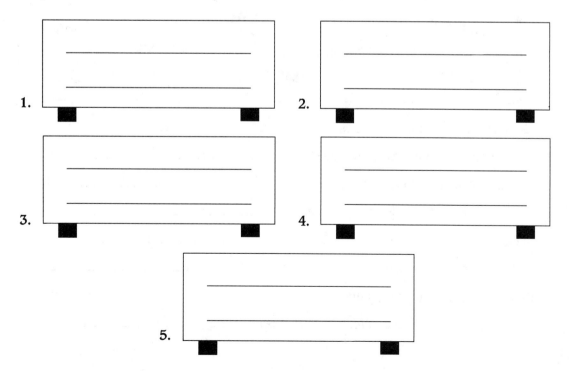

1. _____
2. _____
3. _____
4. _____
5. _____

CAPÍTULO 9 Primer paso

■ SEGUNDO PASO

To ask for help in a store or to talk about how clothes look and fit, you may want to use some department store vocabulary as well as comparisons.

VOCABULARIO   Department store vocabulary   *Pupil's Edition, p. 231*

9 Ricardo is working at a clothing store. Indicate whether his statements are **(P) probable** or **(I) improbable**. If his statements are improbable, change them to make them **probable**.

_____ 1. Sí, señor. Usted puede pagarlo en los probadores allí.

_____

_____ 2. Usted debe pagarle a la cajera que está en el escaparate.

_____

_____ 3. El precio en la etiqueta es veinte dólares.

_____

_____ 4. La cajera pone el dinero en la caja.

_____

_____ 5. Esas botas le quedan muy bien.

_____

_____ 6 Sí, señora. Soy el cliente. Trabajo aquí todos los días.

_____

10 Fill in the blank with the word from the word bank that best completes each sentence.

> escaparate   botas   cliente
> dependiente   etiqueta
> cajera   probadores   par   caja

1. La mujer que ayuda a los clientes es la _____.
2. Un hombre que quiere comprar algo es un _____.
3. Si quiero saber cuánto cuesta algo, miro la _____.
4. Quiero comprar el vestido rojo que vi en el _____.
5. Si quieres probarte el suéter, los _____ están allí.
6. La trabajadora que recibe el dinero del cliente es la _____.
7. Dos botas del mismo tipo y número son un _____ de botas.
8. Los empleados ponen el dinero de los clientes en la _____.

¿Te acuerdas? Comparisons *Pupil's Edition, p. 234*

To compare two things, use **más / menos... que** or **tan... como.**
Este suéter es **más** grande **que** el otro.
Este vestido es **tan** barato **como** la falda.

11 Based on the following store receipts, compare the clothes that Claudette bought with those Laura bought. Use the adjectives in parentheses in your sentences.

MODELO los precios de los vestidos (caro)
El vestido de Claudette es menos caro que el vestido de Laura.

Claudette

Artículo	Precio	Talla
botas	$80,50	7
zapatos	$38,80	5
vestido	$25,00	4
falda	$42,00	6
blusa	$15,00	6

Laura

Artículo	Precio	Talla
botas	$81,00	5
zapatos	$40,00	5
vestido	$30,00	4
falda	$45,00	4
blusa	$15,00	4

1. los precios de las botas (caro)

_____

2. los precios de los zapatos (caro)

_____

3. los precios de las faldas (barato)

_____

4. los precios de las blusas (barato)

_____

5. las tallas de los vestidos (pequeño)

_____

6. las tallas de las faldas (grande)

_____

7. las tallas de las blusas (grande)

_____

8. las tallas de las botas (grande)

_____

CAPÍTULO 9 Segundo paso

◼ TERCER PASO

To bargain in a market you'll need to use direct object pronouns and vocabulary to discuss prices.

VOCABULARIO   Discussing prices   *Pupil's Edition, p. 237*

12 Answer the following questions according to the sales advertised below.

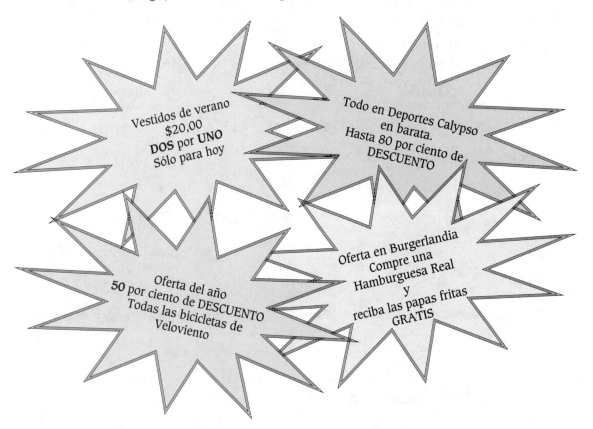

Vestidos de verano
$20,00
DOS por **UNO**
Sólo para hoy

Todo en Deportes Calypso
en barata.
Hasta 80 por ciento de
DESCUENTO

Oferta del año
50 por ciento de DESCUENTO
Todas las bicicletas de
Veloviento

Oferta en Burgerlandia
Compre una
Hamburguesa Real
y
reciba las papas fritas
GRATIS

1. Adriana compró dos vestidos de verano y sólo pagó $20. ¿Por qué?

   _____

2. Una Hamburguesa Real cuesta $2,50. Ana compró una Hamburguesa Real y papas fritas por $2,50. ¿Por qué?

   _____

3. Normalmente una bicicleta *Veloviento XAX* cuesta $300 pero ahora sólo cuesta $150. ¿Qué tipo de descuento ofrecen?

   _____

4. ¿Qué tipo de oferta hay en *Deportes Calypso*?

   _____

5. Beto compró un traje de baño, un básquetbol y una raqueta en *Deportes Calypso*. ¿Por qué compró todo en descuento?

   _____

13 Alejandro is writing his sister Casandra about his trip to the Otavalo Market. Complete his letter with words from the word bank.

| descuento | dos por uno | en barata | ganga |
| por ciento | | gratis | al aire libre |

Casandra,

Me encanta el Ecuador. Ayer fui al mercado (1) _____ de Otavalo. Todos los suéteres estaban (2) _____. En un lugar había un (3) _____ de 40 por ciento. En otro lugar había una oferta de (4) _____. Allí compré un suéter y me dieron el segundo (5) _____. ¡Qué (6) _____!

¿Se te ha olvidado? Direct object pronouns *Pupil's Edition, p. 100*

14 Complete the following phone message that Isabel left Ana by filling in the blanks with the correct direct object pronouns.

Hola, Ana. (1) _____ llamé a ti ayer pero no estabas. Hoy Rosa (2) _____ acompañó al mercado. Compré dos sombreros. El vendedor me (3) _____ dejó en dos por uno. ¡Te van a gustar mis nuevas camisetas! Me (4) _____ regaló por treinta dólares. Rosa y yo compramos unas botas. Nos (5) _____ dio por veinticinco dólares. ¡Qué ganga! Estamos aquí en mi casa. (6) Lláma_____ pronto.

15 Write what you'd ask to find out where these people do the following things.

MODELO Gil siempre busca las mejores gangas en ropa. **¿Dónde las busca?**

1. Ana siempre compra los zapatos de tenis más de moda.

   ¿_____?

2. Andrés y Beto siempre escuchan la música más moderna.

   ¿_____?

3. Lola siempre ve las mejores películas.

   ¿_____?

4. Armando y Pepe siempre encuentran los mejores restaurantes.

   ¿_____?

CAPÍTULO 9 Tercer paso

10 ¡Cuéntame!

■ PRIMER PASO

To set the scene for a story, you may need to use **ser** in the imperfect tense, as well as **oír**, **creer**, **leer**, and **caerse** in the preterite. You'll also need to use the preterite and imperfect in the same sentence. You may want to use reflexive verbs and some weather vocabulary as well.

VOCABULARIO   Weather   *Pupil's Edition, p. 253*

1 Find eight Spanish words in the box below that describe the weather and write them in the appropriate spaces.

```
O  D  Ú  D  R  S  D  Ñ  G  N  U  B  L  A  D  O  G  Y  S  A
R  A  L  N  Í  N  U  B  C  R  Ñ  Y  P  J  G  D  T  A  H  D
E  D  L  G  Y  I  R  A  D  A  S  I  Ú  D  H  L  R  N  Ú  Ú
C  H  O  R  P  E  L  Ú  T  Y  C  A  L  S  L  J  U  G  M  C
A  P  H  Í  H  B  I  S  H  O  D  A  Ú  A  I  P  E  L  E  E
U  S  Ñ  Ú  G  L  D  E  L  H  V  E  S  P  D  A  N  T  D  H
G  I  Y  G  J  A  H  D  N  Í  A  T  N  E  M  R  O  T  O  Ñ
A  L  Ú  A  L  Y  O  D  A  J  E  P  S  E  D  U  R  T  R  Ú
```

1. downpour _____
2. thunder _____
3. clear _____
4. humid _____
5. lightning _____
6. cloudy _____
7. fog _____
8. storm _____

2 Complete Captain O'Mulligan's tall tales by filling in the blanks with words from Activity 1.

1. ¡Era tan _____ que la ropa no se secaba por dos semanas!

2. ¡Había tanta _____ que la gente no podía encontrar sus casas!

3. ¡Estaba tan _____ que se podía ver desde aquí hasta Asia!

4. ¡El _____ hacía tanto ruido como cien trenes!

5. ¡Después del _____ la calle era como el Río Amazonas!

6. ¡Estaba tan _____ que no veíamos el sol!

7. ¡Había tantos _____ que se convertía *(it changed)* la noche en día!

¿Se te ha olvidado?   The imperfect of **ser**   *Pupil's Edition, p. 179*

3 Julio is writing a story about an adventure-filled summer. Complete the beginning of his story with the imperfect of **ser**.

Hace cinco años mi primo Alejandro pasó el verano con mi familia.

Mi hermano Simón (1)_____ muy aventurero, y él y

mi primo (2) _____ buenos amigos.

Yo (3)_____ el menor de la familia pero Alejandro,

Simón y yo siempre hacíamos muchas cosas juntos.

Nosotros (4) _____ bastante traviesos. Un día todo

eso cambió. (5) _____ las cinco de la tarde cuando...

---

*G*ramática   Preterite vs. imperfect   *Pupil's Edition, p. 254*

1. When talking about the past, an action in progress can often be interrupted by some event. In that situation the imperfect expresses the action in progress and the preterite expresses the interrupting event.

   Comían cuando sus amigos **llegaron.**

   They were eating when their friends arrived.

---

4 Complete Karin's story about meeting a famous singer with the imperfect or the preterite of the verbs in parentheses.

Ayer cuando yo **(1)**_____ (esperar) a mi amiga vi a Enrique Iglesias.

Yo estaba en el restaurante Club Miami cuando un hombre **(2)**_____

(entrar). Él se sentó con otro hombre en una mesa cerca de mí. Escuchaba su

conversación cuando el camarero **(3)**_____ (llegar) a mi mesa.

(4)_____ (hablar) con el camarero cuando Enrique se levantó para salir. De

repente me levanté y cuando él pasaba mi mesa le **(5)**_____ (pedir) su

autógrafo. Enrique **(6)**_____ (escribir) su nombre cuando me preguntó si

tenía entradas para el concierto. Le dije que no y me dio dos entradas. ¡Qué suerte!

---

5 Patricia didn't study enough last weekend. Fill in the blanks with the imperfect or the preterite of the verbs in parentheses to find out why.

No estudié mucho anoche. Yo **(1)** _____ (estudiar) historia cuando mi amiga

Silvia me **(2)** _____ (llamar). Nosotros **(3)** _____ (hablar)

de su novio cuando Esteban **(4)** _____ (llegar). Él nos invitó a Silvia y a mí a

comer con él. Luego, nosotros **(5)** _____ (comer) cuando el novio de Silvia

(6) _____ (entrar) en el restaurante. Nos invitó a una fiesta.
Por eso, no pude estudiar.

---

*G*ramática   Preterite vs. imperfect   *Pupil's Edition, p. 254*

2. The imperfect also gives background information about a particular event: the way things were, what was happening, and how people felt.

Llovía muchísimo pero **estaban** muy contentos.

---

6 Combine the following elements to provide the background information to a mystery story.

1. Ser / las ocho / de la noche

_____

2. Carlos / caminar / por el parque

_____

3. Esta vez / Ricardo / no estar / con él

_____

4. Hacer / frío / y / hay / mucha niebla

_____

5. Carlos pensar / que / estar / solo / pero . . .

_____

7 Write a paragraph describing when you met your best friend. Be sure to include where you were, how old you were, what time of day it was, and what you were doing. You should also describe what your best friend was like.

_____

_____

_____

_____

_____

VOCABULARIO   Reflexive verbs   *Pupil's Edition, p. 255*

8 Complete the crossword puzzle using the clues below.

```
   ┌───┬───┬───┬───┬───┬───┬───┐   ┌───┐
   │1  │   │   │2  │   │   │   │   │3  │
   └───┴───┴───┼───┼───┴───┴───┘   ├───┤
               │   │               │   │
               ├───┤   ┌───┬───┬───┤   │
               │   │   │4  │   │   │   │
               ├───┤   └───┴───┴───┴───┘
               │   │
   ┌───┬───┬───┼───┼───┬───┐
   │5  │   │   │   │   │   │
   └───┴───┴───┴───┴───┴───┘
```

Horizontales

1. Mis amigos dicen *¡Hasta luego!* cuando se _____.
4. Normalmente dos personas se enamoran primero y después se _____.
5. Cuando me acuesto tarde, me _____ en clase.

Verticales

2. Siempre me _____ si no uso mapa.
3. Los viernes los empleados salen a las ocho pero hoy se _____ a las siete.
4. Mi hermano se _____ con frecuencia. Ayer se rompió el brazo.

Nota *G*ramatical   Spelling changes in the preterite   *Pupil's Edition, p. 255*

The preterite of **oír, creer, leer,** and **caerse** has the letter *y* in the third person singular and plural.

Los muchachos **oyeron** un ruido misterioso pero el profesor no **oyó** nada.

---

9 Everyone in Samuel's family slept poorly last night. Explain why by completing the sentences with the correct preterite forms of **oír, creer, leer,** and **caerse.**

1. Samuel _____ un ruido raro a las once. _____ que era el perro.

2. La señora Donoso _____ otro ruido a las doce. _____

   que era la gata.

3. El hermano de Samuel _____ su libro de historia casi toda la noche porque

   había un examen en la mañana.

4. Las hermanitas de Samuel _____ una persona en la casa. Unos vasos

   _____ en la cocina.

5. Después de la una de la mañana, ninguno de los Donoso _____ otro ruido

   pero todavía no podían dormir.

■ SEGUNDO PASO

To continue and end a story, you may need some special vocabulary such as that used in science fiction or fairy tales, as well as the preterite and imperfect tenses.

VOCABULARIO   Science fiction and fairy tales   *Pupil's Edition, p. 259*

10 Nuria is telling you her favorite fairy tale. Fill in the blanks with the appropriate words from the word bank. You'll need to know the words **una pata de oro** *(a golden leg)* and **convirtió** *(changed)*.

> enano   príncipe   madrina   estrella
> princesa   hadas   ladrón

Mi cuento de **(1)** _____ favorito dice así:

Érase una vez una **(2)** _____ que se llamaba Carmela. Ella vivía sola en un castillo con su gato que tenía una pata de oro. Un día un **(3)** _____ con una máscara negra entró en el castillo y se robó al gato. Carmela estaba muy triste. En el bosque, un **(4)** _____ de orejas grandes y de estatura muy pequeña vio al hombre malo que tenía el gato de la princesa. Muy rápidamente tomó al gato y corrió hacia el castillo. Allí fue cuando el hada **(5)** _____ convirtió a este hombre pequeño en un **(6)** _____ alto y guapo. Cuando Carmela lo vio, se enamoró de él y al final, se casaron.

11 Fill in the blanks to find out about space and our solar system. Use the vocabulary on page 259 of your textbook.

1. Pluto, Júpiter y Saturno son _____.

2. El sol es la _____ que queda más cerca de nuestro planeta.

3. _____ significa Objeto Volador No Identificado.

4. Una _____ es un grupo de estrellas.

5. El Enterprise es una _____ de NASA.

*G*ramática   The imperfect and preterite to tell a story   *Pupil's Edition, p. 260*

When telling a story, use both the preterite and imperfect tenses.

1. The imperfect tense sets the scene. It tells what was going on and describes people, places, moods, and situations: **Era** una noche oscura...

2. Use an expression such as **un día, de repente,** or **fue cuando** plus a verb in the preterite to tell something that happened: **De repente llegó** un enano...

3. Continue your story with expressions like **entonces, luego,** and **después** plus the preterite: **Luego llegó** la Princesa de Aragón.

4. End the story with the preterite to tell how things came out: ...**y todos vivieron felizmente.**

12 Find out what happens in the following story by choosing the correct verb tense for each sentence and writing the correct form in the blank provided.

1. Érase una vez un planeta donde _____ (vivían, vivieron) unos animales muy grandes.

2. Se cuenta que había una serpiente que _____ (era, fue) gigantesca.

3. Un día la serpiente _____ (se despertaba, se despertó) con sed.

4. Fue cuando ella _____ (se tomaba, se tomó) todos los ríos y lagos.

5. Los otros animales _____ (tenían, tuvieron) sed.

6. Entonces los animales _____ (decidían, decidieron) contarle chistes a la serpiente.

7. Durante horas, los animales le contaron chistes. De repente, la serpiente

_____ (hablaba, habló).

8. Al final, el agua _____ (volvía, volvió) a llenar los océanos.

13 Complete the story of *El castillo de sal* with the correct forms of the verbs in parentheses.

Érase una vez un príncipe que **(1)** _____ (vivir) en un hermoso castillo

de sal. El castillo **(2)** _____ (estar) en las montañas. Nunca

(3) _____ (llover) allí. Un día, el príncipe

(4) _____ (bajar) de la montaña y **(5)** _____ (ver)

un lago por primera vez. "Yo quiero un lago", **(6)** _____ (pensar) el

príncipe. Entonces él y cien enanos **(7)** _____ (llevar) el lago a la

montaña. Una mañana, de repente, el agua del lago **(8)** _____ (llegar)

al castillo y el castillo de sal **(9)** _____ (caerse). Al final, el príncipe

(10) _____ (perder) su casa.

14 Complete this story by combining the following elements. Use either the imperfect or the preterite tense.

1. Hace mucho tiempo / vivir / una tortuga / en la selva

2. La tortuga / ser / el animal más rápido de la selva

3. Un día / llegar / un loro

4. El loro / creer / que poder / correr más rápido que la tortuga

5. Los animales / decidir / hacer una carrera *(race)*

6. Empezar / la competencia / a las seis / de la mañana

7. El loro / terminar / de primero y la tortuga de segundo

8. Al final la tortuga / decidir / ser el animal más lento de la selva

15 Make up your own story by completing the following sentences.

1. Érase una vez una mujer que _____

2. Su casita _____

3. Un día un ladrón _____

4. El ladrón _____

5. De repente el príncipe _____

6. Luego el ladrón _____

7. Al final, la mujer y el príncipe _____

■ TERCER PASO

To talk about and react to the latest news, you'll need to use some specific vocabulary. You may also need to use the verb **tener** in the preterite.

VOCABULARIO   Talking about the news   *Pupil's Edition, p. 262*

16 Unscramble the words that correspond to the definitions below.

1. Una persona que habla de otras personas sin saber si la información es verdad.

    S   O   M   H   O   I   C   S _____

2. Lo que lees en el periódico.

    T   N   C   O   I   I   S   A _____

3. Otra palabra para *enojado.*

    R   O   U   F   I   O   S _____

4. Lo opuesto de *hacer las paces.*

    R   R   P   O   E   M   O   N   C _____

5. Información que no es necesariamente la verdad.

    H   M   E   C   I   S   _____

17 Geraldo is writing Carolina a note. Complete his note with the words below.

metiche	romper	chismoso
hacer las paces	furioso	chisme

Carolina,

¿Has oído que Diana y José pelearon durante la fiesta anoche? Ella

quería **(1)** _____ con él porque ella lo vio con Elena.

No sé si es un **(2)** _____ o es la verdad, pero Carla me

dijo que Juan le dijo que José estaba **(3)** _____ con

Diana. Pero, ¿quién sabe? Juan es un **(4)** _____.

Le encanta hablar de otras personas. De todos modos, me dijo que

Patricia trató de ayudarles a **(5)** _____ pero ahora

están enojados con Patricia por ser **(6)** _____.

Bueno, te escribo más tarde.

Geraldo

Nota Gramatical   The preterite of **tener**   *Pupil's Edition, p. 264*

The preterite of **tener** is irregular.

yo	**tuve**	nosotros	**tuvimos**
tú	**tuviste**	vosotros	tuvisteis
él / ella / usted	**tuvo**	ellos / ellas / ustedes	**tuvieron**

18 Complete the following sensational headlines with the preterite forms of **tener.**

1. ¡Pasamos dos meses sin agua y no _____ sed!

2. ¿Alguna vez _____ tú un hada madrina? ¡Ahora sí!

3. Vi el OVNI y _____ ganas de ir con ellos.

4. Princesa y príncipe _____ problemas en España.

5. Ladrón _____ suerte. Perro nunca se despertó.

19 Beatriz is telling Paco about the latest news. Based on Paco's reactions, write the questions she asked, using expressions from page 263 of your textbook.

MODELO   **¿Has oído que tuvimos que salir temprano?**
         ¿De veras? ¿Ustedes tuvieron que salir temprano?

1. ¿ _____?
   ¡No me digas! ¿Tuviste una cita con Roberto?

2. ¿ _____?
   ¿De veras? ¿Ustedes tuvieron que hablar con el director?

3. ¿ _____?
   ¿Tú crees? ¿Simón sólo tuvo dos días de vacaciones?

4. ¿ _____?
   ¡No lo puedo creer! ¿Ellos no tuvieron que tomar el examen?

5. ¿ _____?
   No, yo no tuve que trabajar.

CAPÍTULO 11

Nuestro medio ambiente

■ PRIMER PASO

To describe a problem, you may need to make negative statements as well as talk about nature and the environment.

VOCABULARIO   The environment   *Pupil's Edition, p. 281*

1 Read the problems listed in each box, and write the cause of each problem in the blank provided. Use the vocabulary on page 281 of your textbook.

1.

> Me duelen los ojos cuando visito a mi tío en la Ciudad de México. También es difícil respirar.

2.

> No hay tantos árboles ahora como antes. Eso causa la muerte de muchos tipos de insectos y animales.

3.

> Ya no podemos pescar donde vivo porque hay petróleo en el agua.

4.

> La gasolina es mucho más cara que antes y no hay suficiente gasolina para todos.

2 Catalina is writing an article about the environment for her school paper. Complete her article using the vocabulary on page 281 of your textbook.

> Nosotros tenemos que evitar los problemas del (1) _____.
>
> En nuestras ciudades es difícil respirar porque hay mucha
>
> (2) _____. En algunas ciudades es imposible ver los edificios
>
> grandes por el (3) _____ y los químicos en el aire contribuyen
>
> a la destrucción de la (4) _____. Y las fábricas tiran muchos
>
> (5) _____ en la basura y contaminan la tierra y el agua.
>
> Tenemos que buscar la (6) _____ ahora. ¡Nuestro futuro
>
> comienza hoy!

Nota *G*ramatical Double negatives *Pupil's Edition, p. 282*

- You may use more than one negative word or expression in a sentence:
  No vino **nadie** a la fiesta de Magalí.
- When **nunca, ninguno, nadie,** or **tampoco** precedes the verb, **no** is left out.
  Nadie vino a la fiesta de Magalí.
- Some other negative words you can use are **nada, ni... ni, nunca, ninguno/a,** and **tampoco**. **Ninguno** shortens to **ningún** before a masculine, singular noun.
  No tengo **ningún** libro sobre la historia de Francia.

3 Unscramble the following sentences to find out about problems that affect our environment.

1. tirar / debemos / ningún / en la basura / químico / no

_____

2. nadie / contaminar / debe / los océanos

_____

3. el smog / ni / la destrucción de las selvas / ni / es bueno

_____

4. tirar / debemos / tampoco / el plástico en la basura / no

_____

5. no / muchas fábricas / hacen / para / evitar / nada / la contaminación

_____

4 Ana and her brother Beto never agree on anything. Based on Ana's opinions about the environment, write what Beto thinks.

MODELO   ANA Podemos hacer <u>algo</u> para el medio ambiente.
         BETO **No podemos hacer nada para el medio ambiente.**

ANA   <u>Todos</u> separan la basura.

BETO **(1)** _____

ANA   <u>Siempre</u> podemos evitar los problemas del smog.

BETO **(2)** No _____

ANA   <u>También</u> podemos evitar la contaminación del mar.

BETO **(3)** _____

ANA   <u>Alguien</u> puede hacer <u>algo</u> para mejorar la situación.

BETO **(4)** _____

ANA   <u>Algún día</u> vamos a vivir en un lugar sin contaminación.

BETO **(5)** _____

¡Ven conmigo! Level 2, Chapter 11

CAPÍTULO 11 Primer paso

5 Answer the following questions about your city or a city near you.

1. ¿Hay mucha contaminación del aire en tu ciudad?

   _____

2. ¿Tira mucha gente plástico en la basura?

   _____

3. ¿Hay mucho ruido en tu ciudad?

   _____

4. ¿Notas muchos efectos de la destrucción de la capa de ozono?

   _____

5. ¿Qué podemos hacer para mejorar la situación?

   _____

VOCABULARIO   Animals   *Pupil's Edition, p. 283*

6 Decide which animals from page 283 of your textbook are most affected by air pollution and which are most affected by water pollution. Then write the name of each animal in the appropriate column.

La contaminación del aire	**La contaminación del mar**
_____	_____
_____	_____
_____	_____
_____	_____

7 Complete the crossword puzzle using the clues provided.

Horizontales

3. Puede ser un vampiro.

5. La gente pesca los _____.

6. El animal más grande del mar.

Verticales

1. Animales inteligentes que viven en el mar.

2. Símbolo de los Estados Unidos.

4. El mosquito es un tipo de _____.

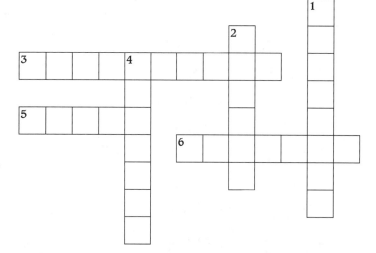

CAPÍTULO 11   Primer paso

■ SEGUNDO PASO

To talk about consequences, you'll need to use phrases such as **por lo tanto, por eso,** and **por consiguiente.** To express agreement and disagreement, you'll need to use certain idiomatic expressions.

 **ASÍ SE DICE**   Talking about consequences   *Pupil's Edition, p. 288*

8 Felipe is president of the **Club Tierra Verde**, and tonight he's giving a speech at your school. Help him out by filling in the blanks with appropriate words from page 288 of your textbook.

> Cuando yo era niño vivía cerca de un bosque. **(1)** _____
>
> eso me encantan los árboles. Hoy, ese bosque es un campo de golf.
>
> Por lo **(2)** _____ formé esta organización hace un año.
>
> Creo que es **(3)** _____ hacer algo para cuidar los
>
> bosques. Tenemos que **(4)** _____ esta crisis ecológica.

 **ASÍ SE DICE**   Expressing agreement and disagreement   *Pupil's Edition, p. 289*

9 Here's how Felipe's schoolmates reacted to his suggestion that seniors should be allowed to go to the head of the lunch line. Indicate whether each person agreed or disagreed by placing a check mark in the appropriate column.

		Sí	No
1. LAURA	"Así es la cosa."		
2. ARMANDO	"¡Te equivocas!"		
3. ALICIA	"¡Al contrario!"		
4. RAMÓN	"¡Claro que sí!"		
5. MAURICIO	"No me parece."		
6. RAQUEL	"Sin duda alguna."		
7. ROSARIO	"¡Eso es!"		
8. ANTONIO	"Tienes razón."		

CAPÍTULO 11 Segundo paso

10 Several students have formed an ecology club but they can't agree on what its focus should be. Complete the following conversation with the appropriate words from the word bank.

razón	equivocas	siento	contrario	siento
parece		acuerdo	punto	así	eso

EDUARDO   Creo que los científicos deberían inventar nuevas formas de energía.

GABRIELA   Sí, estoy de **(1)** _____. Los carros, por ejemplo, deberían usar solamente energía solar.

SYLVIA   Lo **(2)** _____, pero no me **(3)** _____. Creo que la contaminación del agua es el problema más grave.

HÉCTOR   Sí, tienes **(4)** _____. El verano pasado nosotros no pudimos nadar.

SYLVIA   **(5)** _____ es la cosa. Y cuando queremos ir a pescar no podemos porque el agua está contaminada. Nuestro club debería proteger las aguas.

GABRIELA   ¡Al **(6)** _____! Nuestro club debería hacer algo sobre la contaminación del aire.

SYLVIA   ¡Te **(7)** _____! La contaminación del agua es más importante.

EDUARDO   Hasta cierto **(8)** _____ todos ustedes tienen razón. ¿Qué tal si llamamos nuestro club Contra Contaminación — del aire y del agua?

GABRIELA   ¡**(9)** _____ es!

11 Indicate whether you agree or disagree with the following statements and explain why. Be sure to use the expressions on page 289 of your textbook.

MODELO   El mayor problema del medio ambiente es el ruido.
No estoy de acuerdo. El mayor problema del ambiente es la contaminación del aire.

1. La pesca de los delfines no es un problema grave.

_____

_____

2. La contaminación del mar no es un problema grave.

_____

_____

3. Debemos tirar el plástico y los periódicos en la basura.

_____

_____

4. No podemos hacer nada para evitar los problemas del medio ambiente.

_____

_____

■ TERCER PASO

To talk about obligations and solutions, you may want to use some cognates. You may want to use affirmative words and refer to environmental issues. You may also need to use **si** clauses, **nosotros** commands, and informal commands.

¿Se te ha olvidado?   Cognates   *Pupil's Edition, p. 49*

12 Read the following bulletin board posting and circle ten cognates. Then write each one and its English equivalent in the space provided.

> Con un poquito de cooperación, todos nosotros podemos mejorar la situación. Podemos salvar a los animales en peligro de extinción, eliminar la destrucción de las selvas tropicales y conservar la energía. ¡A todos nosotros nos toca hacer algo!

1. _____   6. _____
2. _____   7. _____
3. _____   8. _____
4. _____   9. _____
5. _____   10. _____

¿Te acuerdas?   Affirmative words   *Pupil's Edition, p. 292*

13 Based on the responses given, write the questions that were asked. Be sure to use **siempre**, **algo**, and **alguien** in your responses.

1. ¿ _____?
   No, no tiro nada de plástico en la basura.

2. ¿ _____?
   No, no conozco a nadie en una organización ecológica.

3. ¿ _____?
   No, nunca apago la luz cuando salgo de mi cuarto.

4. ¿ _____?
   No, no sé nada de las aves en peligro de extinción.

5. ¿ _____?
   No, no hablo con nadie sobre los problemas del medio ambiente.

VOCABULARIO Environmental issues *Pupil's Edition, p. 293*

14 Complete the following proposal to make your school more environmentally responsible.

Para conservar la **(1)** _____, debemos **(2)** _____ las luces cuando salimos de las clases. Debemos evitar los productos **(3)** _____ y **(4)** _____ limpia nuestra escuela. Necesitamos participar en un programa de **(5)** _____ también. Debemos **(6)** _____ los productos de aluminio y de vidrio.

15 Propose a solution to each of the following problems using the vocabulary you've learned.

MODELO El desperdicio del petróleo es un problema grave.
Hay que conservar nuestros recursos naturales.

1. No sé qué hacer con todas esas latas de aluminio.

_____

2. Hay muchos animales en peligro de extinción.

_____

3. Hay mucha basura en los parques de la ciudad.

_____

4. Gastamos mucha electricidad en nuestra casa.

_____

*N*ota *G*ramatical Si clauses *Pupil's Edition, p. 293*

The word **si** *(if)* can be used with a verb in the present tense to talk about what will or may happen under certain conditions.
Si trabajamos juntos, podemos resolver los problemas.

16 Unscramble the following sentences to see what can happen if we all work together.

1. los carros / el smog / si no usamos / podemos eliminar / todos los días

_____

2. tiramos / si evitamos / menos basura / los productos empacados

_____

3. mantener limpia / si reciclamos / la ciudad / podemos

_____

4. más energía / las luces/ conservamos / si apagamos

_____

5. la situación / nuestro estilo de vida / mejoramos / si cambiamos

_____

17 Combine the elements and complete the sentences to indicate the possible consequences of each situation.

MODELO   Si / (nosotros) trabajar / juntos...
   Si trabajamos juntos podemos mejorar la situación.

1. Si / (nosotros) conservar / energía...

   _____

2. Si / (nosotros) eliminar / las selvas tropicales...

   _____

3. Si / (nosotros) no proteger / las especies...

   _____

4. Si / (nosotros) no eliminar / el smog...

   _____

Gramática   **Nosotros** commands   *Pupil's Edition, p. 294*

- **Nosotros** commands express the idea of *"Let's . . ."*
- To form **nosotros** commands, add -**mos** to the **usted** command forms.
   ¡Conserve**mos** energía!
   ¡Cuide**mos** el medio ambiente!

18 Andrea's ecology club is making posters. Make the following slogans involve everyone in the school by rewriting them with **nosotros** commands.

¡Recicle el aluminio, las latas y el vidrio!	1. _____
¡Venga al colegio a pie o en bicicleta!	2. _____
¡Mantenga limpias las calles!	3. _____
Al salir del baño, apague las luces.	4. _____
Sean más responsables.	5. _____

19 Using **nosotros** commands, indicate whether we should or shouldn't do the following things.

1. cambiar nuestro estilo de vida

   _____

2. evitar los productos empacados

   _____

3. desperdiciar el petróleo

   _____

4. tirar productos químicos en la basura

   _____

5. mantener limpias nuestras ciudades

   _____

20 Answer the following questions using **nosotros** commands.

MODELO   Hay mucho smog en nuestra ciudad. ¿Qué hacemos?
         Tomemos el metro y dejemos el carro en casa.

1. A muchas personas no les interesa la naturaleza. ¿Qué podemos hacer?

   _____

2. Cada día hay menos selvas tropicales. ¿Qué hacemos?

   _____

3. El mar está muy contaminado. ¿Qué hacemos?

   _____

4. La gente no sabe dónde tirar la basura. ¿Qué podemos hacer nosotros?

   _____

5. Las tortugas marinas están en peligro de extinción. ¿Qué hacemos?

   _____

¿Se te ha olvidado?   Informal commands   *Pupil's Edition, p. 123*

21 Using informal commands, write five things you would advise a friend to do to help the environment.

   _____

   _____

   _____

   _____

   _____

   _____

CAPÍTULO 11 Tercer paso

Veranos pasados, veranos por venir

■ PRIMER PASO

To exchange the latest news, you may want to use some phrases that are often used in letters. To talk about where you went and what you did, you may want to use some specific vocabulary, as well as the preterite tense.

VOCABULARIO   Writing letters   *Pupil's Edition, p. 307*

1 Imagine you're writing a letter to a friend. Choose the items from the word bank that you would use to express the following things.

> Con cariño...   Gracias por...   Te echo mucho de menos.
>
> Un abrazo de...   Querido/a...   Dale un saludo de mi parte.

1. Love . . . _____
2. Dear . . . _____
3. I really miss you. _____
4. Tell him hello from me. _____
5. A hug from . . . _____

2 Read Begonia's letter and fill in the blanks with the correct vocabulary words.

> *(1) _____ Lorenzo,*
> *¿Cómo estás, chico? Te (2) _____ mucho de (3) _____.*
> *Hace mucho tiempo que no te veo... tienes que llamarme pronto.*
> *(4) _____ por el disco compacto que me mandaste para mi cumpleaños.*
> *Me encanta la música de "Los chimpancés locos". Y, por favor, (5) _____*
> *un (6) _____ a tu mamá de mi parte y dile que espero verla pronto.*
> *Un (7) _____ de tu amiga,*
> *   Begonia*

3 Write a short note to a friend who lives in another city. Begin with an appropriate salutation. Then tell your friend you miss him or her and ask your friend to say hello to someone for you. Close your letter with an appropriate phrase and sign your name.

_____

_____

_____

_____

_____

VOCABULARIO   Things you did   *Pupil's Edition, p. 308*

4 Using the vocabulary on page 308 of your textbook, complete Lenny's sentences about what he and his friends did last summer. Conjugate all verbs in the preterite tense.

1. Yo _____ en tabla de vela casi todos los fines de semana.

2. Mario y yo _____ empleos en el Supermercado Super Gigante.

3. Gene y Raquel _____ en casa y leyeron mucho.

4. Carolyn se quedó unas semanas en un _____ juvenil en Europa.

5. Y tú _____ con unos parientes, ¿no?

5 Read each person's plans for last summer. Then use a phrase from the phrase bank to write a sentence describing what each person did. Use the preterite tense.

MODELO   Humberto quería trabajar como voluntario en su ciudad.
Se hizo amigo de muchas personas en su ciudad.

> quedarse con unos parientes   hacerse amigo/a de muchas personas en su ciudad
>
> quedarse en casa   quedarse en un albergue juvenil   montar en tabla de vela
>
> encontrar un empleo

1. Mario quería conocer a jóvenes de otras ciudades y países.

_____

2. Chely tenía ganas de descansar y pasar más tiempo con su familia.

_____

3. Magaly pensaba trabajar y ganar un poco de dinero.

_____

4. Alfredo quería viajar para ver a sus abuelos y a sus tíos.

_____

5. Lily quería ir al lago todos los días.

_____

CAPÍTULO 12 Primer paso

¿Se te ha olvidado? The preterite *Pupil's Edition, p. 353*

MONTAR		CONOCER		ESCRIBIR	
mont**é**	mont**amos**	conoc**í**	conoc**imos**	escrib**í**	escrib**imos**
mont**aste**	montasteis	conoc**iste**	conocisteis	escrib**iste**	escribisteis
mont**ó**	mont**aron**	conoc**ió**	conoc**ieron**	escrib**ió**	escrib**ieron**

6 Here are some responses to a survey about what people did during their last vacation. Based on each response, write the question that was probably asked.

1. ¿_____?
   —No, no monté en tabla de vela.

2. ¿_____?
   —Sí, encontré un trabajo excelente... en la oficina de una abogada.

3. ¿_____?
   —Sí, conocimos a muchísima gente nueva durante nuestras vacaciones.

4. ¿_____?
   —No, mis hermanos no se quedaron en un albergue juvenil.

5. ¿_____?
   —Sí, escribí muchas cartas a todos mis amigos y a mis parientes en San Diego.

6. ¿_____?
   —No, mi hermana no asistió a clases de arte.

7. ¿_____?
   —Sí, comí mucho. ¡Creo que necesito hacer más ejercicio!

7 Answer the following questions about what you did last summer.

1. ¿Te quedaste mucho en casa con tu familia?

   _____

2. ¿Conociste a mucha gente de otros países?

   _____

3. ¿Te inscribiste en una clase de arte, de música o de ejercicios aeróbicos?

   _____

4. ¿Escuchaste música con tus amigos o amigas?

   _____

5. ¿Corriste un kilómetro todos los días?

   _____

◼ SEGUNDO PASO

To describe people and places in the past, you'll need to use the imperfect tense.

¿Se te ha olvidado?   The regular imperfect   *Pupil's Edition, p. 172*

8 Complete Geraldo's letter to his pen pal with the imperfect tense of the verbs in parentheses.

> *Querida María,*
>
> *Me acuerdo que en julio siempre (1) _____ (estar) nevando y*
> *(2) _____ (hacer) mucho frío. Todos los días mis hermanos y yo*
> *(3) _____ (esquiar) en Bariloche. Cada noche nosotros*
> *(4) _____ (llegar) cansados y (5) _____ (tener) ham-*
> *bre. Mi familia siempre (6) _____ (comer) en el restaurante El Gaucho.*
> *Mis hermanos (7) _____ (pedir) churrasco pero yo (8) _____*
> *(querer) empanadas, mi plato favorito. De niña tú (9) _____ (vivir)*
> *cerca de Bariloche, ¿no? Escríbeme pronto.*
>
> *Besos y abrazos,*
>
> *Geraldo*

9 Verónica is interviewing her grandfather to find out about his childhood. Based on his responses, write the questions Verónica asked.

1. ¿_____?
   Mi familia y yo vivíamos en Bolivia.

2. ¿_____?
   Yo tenía diez años cuando fui a Costa Rica.

3. ¿_____?
   Mi mejor amigo en Costa Rica se llamaba José.

4. ¿_____?
   Yo asistía a clases de lunes a sábado.

5. ¿_____?
   Yo me levantaba a las seis para ir a la escuela.

CAPÍTULO 12 Segundo paso

Nombre _____ Clase _____ Fecha _____

 **¿Se te ha olvidado?**   The imperfect of **ir** and **ver**   *Pupil's Edition, p. 173*

10 Using the imperfect tense, combine the following elements to find out where these people used to go and who or what they used to see during their summer vacations.

1. Ben y Carmen / ir / a Puerto Rico / y / ver / a su tío

   _____

2. Maribel / ir / a Chicago / y / ver / a su familia

   _____

3. Rafa y yo / ir / a Ecuador / y / ver / a muchos turistas

   _____

4. Tú / ir / a California / y / ver / a Ignacio, ¿no?

   _____

5. Yo / ir / a Texas / y / ver / los murciélagos de Austin

   _____

¿Se te ha olvidado?   The imperfect of **ser**   *Pupil's Edition, p. 179*

11 Fill in the blanks with the imperfect tense of ser to find out the answer to the following riddle.

Yo **(1)** _____ un cantante muy famoso. Mi familia y yo **(2)** _____

de Misisipí. De adulto vivía en Tennessee. Mi casa **(3)** _____ muy grande.

Mis canciones de rock **(4)** _____ muy populares. Tú **(5)** _____

bastante joven cuando hicieron estampillas con mi imagen. ¿Quién soy?

                    Soy _____ .

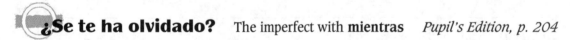 **¿Se te ha olvidado?**   The imperfect with **mientras**   *Pupil's Edition, p. 204*

12 Complete the following sentences to describe your day at school.

1. Yo estaba en la clase de español mientras mi mejor amigo/a _____

   _____ .

2. Yo hacía las tareas mientras mis vecinos _____ .

3. Tú escribías en la pizarra mientras nosotros _____ .

4. Mientras mi director/a comía en la cafetería yo _____ .

5. Mientras llovía yo _____ .

102 Grammar and Vocabulary Workbook, Teacher's Edition

¡Ven conmigo! Level 2, Chapter 12

Copyright © by Holt, Rinehart and Winston. All rights reserved.

¿Se te ha olvidado?   Preterite vs. imperfect   *Pupil's Edition, p. 254*

13 Combine the following elements to indicate what the members of the Ramírez family were doing when they were interrupted.

MODELO   José / hablar / por teléfono / María / llegar / a casa
José hablaba por teléfono cuando María llegó a casa.

1. La señora Ramírez / leer / el periódico / oír / un ruido

_____

2. Los niños / jugar / en el jardín / empezar / a llover

_____

3. El abuelo / dormir / el perro / saltar / encima de la cama

_____

4. Darío / hacer / tarea / el vecino / llamar

_____

5. Nosotros / ver / televisión / Luisito / apagar / las luces

_____

6. Sara / tocar / el piano / su hermano / entrar

_____

7. Yo / poner / la mesa / un vaso / caerse

_____

14 Complete the following paragraph by filling in the blanks with the preterite or imperfect forms of the verbs in parentheses.

EXTRATERRESTRES VISITAN BOLIVIA PARA IR DE COMPRAS

El lunes pasado Manuel Duarte (**1**) _____ (lavar) su carro cuando

(**2**) _____ (ver) un OVNI. La nave espacial (**3**) _____

(ser) muy grande y (**4**) _____ (tener) miles de luces. El señor

Duarte (**5**) _____ (examinar) la nave cuando la puerta se

(**6**) _____ (abrir) y dos hombrecitos (**7**) _____ (salir)

con bolsas de papel. Ellos sólo (**8**) _____ (querer) comprar ponchos

de alpaca porque en su planeta (**9**) _____ (hacer) mucho frío.

CAPÍTULO 12 Segundo paso

■ TERCER PASO

To say when you're going to do something, you'll need to use some specific expressions of time as well as **ir a** + *infinitive.* You'll also need to be familiar with the subjunctive.

 **ASÍ SE DICE**   Saying when you're going   *Pupil's Edition, p. 316*
to do something

15 It's the beginning of June, and Inés is starting her summer vacation. Number the sentences 1 to 5 in the order the events will occur.

_____ **a.** Dentro de un mes vamos a ir a la casa de mi abuela.

_____ **b.** Voy a llamar inmediatamente a mis amigos para hacer planes.

_____ **c.** Cuando vuelva al colegio voy a contarles de mis vacaciones a todos.

_____ **d.** Para fines de agosto voy a comprar ropa para el primer día de clases.

_____ **e.** La semana que viene mi familia y yo pensamos ir a la playa.

16 Complete the crossword puzzle using the clues below.

Horizontales

3. _____ significa *ahora mismo* o *muy pronto.*

6. La película va a empezar muy

_____ , dentro de cinco minutos.

Verticales

1. Estamos en julio. El mes que _____ es agosto.

2. _____ fines de diciembre vamos a esquiar.

4. _____ de un mes vamos a estar de vacaciones.

5. _____ día quiero viajar a España.

¿Se te ha olvidado? Ir a + *infinitive* *Pupil's Edition, p. 354*

17 Roberto is talking about what chores he and his family are going to do. Complete his sentences using ir a + *infinitive* and a direct object pronoun.

MODELO   No pude lavar los platos. **Los voy a lavar** más tarde.

1. Luis no hizo la tarea. _____ cuando vuelva del gimnasio.

2. Ana y Luis no sacaron la basura. Mañana _____ .

3. Patricia y yo no regamos el jardín. _____ el lunes que viene.

4. Ana no lavó los platos. _____ pasado mañana.

5. Yo no ordené mi cuarto. Algún día _____ .

6. ¿No compraste helado, mamá? ¿Cuándo _____ ?

18 Wendy answered a questionnaire about post-graduation plans. Based on her responses, write the questions she answered.

1. ¿_____ ?
No, no voy a vivir con mis padres.

2. ¿_____ ?
Mis padres van a pagar mis estudios.

3. ¿_____ ?
Sí, mis amigos y yo vamos a asistir a la universidad.

4. ¿_____ ?
Vamos a estudiar la literatura española.

5. ¿_____ ?
Vamos a ser maestros de español.

19 What do you think you'll be doing in ten years? Answer the following questions.

1. ¿Dónde vas a vivir?

_____

2. ¿En qué vas a trabajar?

_____

3. ¿Cuánto dinero vas a ganar?

_____

4. ¿Qué tipo de carro vas a tener?

_____

5. ¿Cómo van a ser tus amigos?

_____

CAPÍTULO 12 Tercer paso

VOCABULARIO   Future plans   *Pupil's Edition, p. 316*

20 Complete the following sentences based on your future plans.

1. Cuando termine las clases _____

2. Cuando encuentre un empleo _____

3. Cuando tenga más dinero _____

4. Cuando llegue el otoño _____

Nota *G*ramatical   The subjunctive mood   *Pupil's Edition, p. 316*

In the phrase **cuando vuelva**, the verb **vuelva** is in the subjunctive mood. Notice that the **yo**, **él**, **ella**, and **usted** forms of the subjunctive are the same as the **usted** command form.

hablar → ¡**Hable** Ud. español!

Cuando **hable** mejor el español voy a ir a México.

---

21 In the blanks provided, list all of the subjunctive verbs in the following paragraph.

Dentro de un año me voy a graduar. Cuando me gradúe voy a trabajar con mi padre. Mi amiga Beatriz va a asistir a la Universidad de California inmediatamente. Cuando ella llegue a California va a vivir con sus tíos. Mi amigo Rodolfo va a viajar a Europa cuando termine las clases. Cuando regrese él, sin duda alguna va a hablar cinco idiomas. Yo también voy a aprender muchos idiomas cuando asista a la universidad. ¿Y cuándo voy a ir? Pues, cuando tenga más dinero.

1. _____   4. _____
2. _____   5. _____
3. _____   6. _____

¡Ven conmigo! Level 2, Chapter 12

Answers

Chapter 1

1 1. tengo   2. Tiene   3. tienen
    4. tenemos   5. tienes   6. tienen

2 *Answers will vary.*

3 1. difícil   2. simpática   3. atlética
    4. tímida   5. excelente

4 *Answers will vary.*

5 1. Es mexicano   2. No es habladora
    3. Es española   4. Es italiano
    5. No es colombiana

6 1. franceses   2. viejos   3. calvos
    4. habladores   5. fuertes   6. artísticas

7 *Verticales:* 1. colombiana
    2. guatemalteco   3. uruguaya
    5. hondureña
    Horizontales: 4. ecuatoriana
    6. mexicanos   7. paraguaya
    8. dominicano

8 1. Es panameño Rubén Blades
    2. Es estadounidense Tish Hinojosa
    3. Es cubano Iván Hernández
    4. Es chilena Isabel Allende
    5. Es peruano Mario Vargas Llosa

9 1. tocan   2. canto   3. miramos
    4. comemos   5. escribe

10 1. escribe   2. nadan   3. escuchamos
    4. como, tomo   5. asistes   6. lavan

11 1. haces   2. Voy   3. sales   4. Salgo
    5. vienes   6. Vengo   7. Ven
    8. vemos

12 *Answers will vary.*

13 1. voy a estudiar   2. va a correr
    3. van a ver   4. voy a estar
    5. vamos a leer

14 1. Voy a hacer la tarea.
    2. Vamos a comer en el Café Triomphe.
    3. Va a escribir en su diario.
    4. Van a escuchar la radio.
    5. Y tú vas a jugar al tenis.

15 *Answers will vary.*

16 1. gusta   2. gusta   3. gustan
    4. gustan   5. gusta   6. gustan
    7. gusta   8. gustan

17 *Answers will vary.*

18 1. me   2. Te   3. me   4. le   5. le
    6. nos   7. les   8. nos   9. nos

19 *Answers will vary.*

Chapter 2

1 1. estoy   2. están   3. Estás   4. está
    5. estamos

2 1. Robertín está muy aburrido.
    2. Mis padres están tristes.
    3. Yo estoy nerviosa.
    4. Verónica y yo estamos ocupadas.
    5. Mi padre está enfadado.

3 1. Elena está ocupada.
    2. Rafael está triste.
    3. José Luis y Alejo están aburridos.
    4. Nosotros estamos cansados.

4 1. feliz   2. deprimido   3. emocionado
    4. de mal humor

5 1. Roberto está emocionado.
    2. Claudia está triste.
    3. Mario está aburrido.
    4. El Sr. Obregón está tranquilo.
    5. Están enfermos.

6 1. e   2. d   3. c   4. b   5. a

7 1. El lunes pasado compró su boleto.
    2. Anteayer fue al Banco Central.
    3. Ayer por la mañana lavó la ropa.
    4. Anoche hizo las maletas.
    5. Esta mañana llamó un taxi.

8 1. llegamos   2. bucearon
    3. tomamos   4. regresó   5. bailé

9 1. visitamos el mercado Libertad
    2. no tomé muchas fotos
    3. no mandé las postales
    4. compramos regalos para nuestros
      amigos

10 *Answers will vary.*

11 1. fuimos   2. fue   3. fui   4. fuimos
    5. fue   6. fui

12 1. muchos libros
    2. unas tiendas de ropa
    3. una película cómica
    4. el arte de Botero
    5. unos animales exóticos

13 1. fuimos a un baile
    2. fueron al correo
    3. fui a la biblioteca
    4. fueron al cine
    5. fuiste al centro comercial

Answers

14 1. quiero, puedo   2. quieren, pueden
     3. queremos, podemos   4. quiere, puede
     5. quiere, puede   6. quieres, puedes

15 1. estamos   2. están   3. están
     4. están   5. estamos   6. está
     7. está   8. están

16 1. Dónde estás
     2. Dónde están tus padres
     3. Dónde estamos nosotros
     4. Dónde está tu carro
     5. Dónde están mis libros

17 1. d   2. a   3. c   4. b

18 1. llueve y hace fresco.
     2. llueve y hace frío.
     3. hace sol y calor.
     4. hace sol y fresco.
     5. llueve y hace frío.
     6. nieva y hace frío.

19 *Answers will vary.*

Chapter 3

1 1. el peine   2. levantarse   3. el jabón
     4. vestirse

2 1. el despertador   2. el champú
     3. la secadora de pelo
     4. la pasta de dientes   5. me miro

3 1. ducharse   2. peinarse
     3. lavarse los dientes   4. maquillarse
     5. afeitarse

4 1. se despiertan   2. nos levantamos
     3. me ducho, me lavo   4. se baña
     5. se seca   6. nos lavamos

5 1. me levanto   2. levantarse
     3. bañarse   4. me baño
     5. despertarse   6. despertarnos
     7. se acuestan   8. acostarte

6 1. nos vestimos   2. se visten
     3. se viste   4. me visto   5. se viste
     6. vestirte

7 *Answers will vary.*

8 1. la cocina   2. tender la cama
     3. pasar la aspiradora   4. poner la mesa
     5. cortar

9 1. Ordenas tu cuarto todos los días
     2. Quién saca la basura
     3. Riegan tus padres el jardín los fines de semana
     4. Pone la mesa tu padre
     5. Limpian el cuarto de baño tus hermanos o tus hermanas
     6. Tienden tú y tu familia las camas

10 1. Tu cuarto, ¿lo ordenaste?
     2. El césped, ¿lo cortaste?
     3. La mesa, ¿la quitaste?
     4. Los platos, ¿los lavaste?
     5. La aspiradora, ¿la pasaste?

11 *Answers will vary.*

12 *Answers will vary.*

13 *Answers will vary.*

14 1. d   2. a   3. b   4. e   5. c

15 1. trabajar en mecánica
     2. tocar con la banda
     3. juegan a las cartas
     4. reunirse con sus amigos
     5. Hace monopatín

16 *Answers will vary.*

17 1. acampar   2. pescar   3. bucear
     4. leer tiras cómicas   5. juego videojuegos

18 *Answers will vary.*

19 1. hace   2. Hace   3. hace   4. que

20 1. Cuánto tiempo hace que es actriz, Hace cinco años que es actriz.
     2. Cuánto tiempo hace que escribe poemas, Hace diez años que escribe poemas.
     3. Cuánto tiempo hace que vive en Monterrey, Hace cinco meses que vive en Monterrey.

Chapter 4

1 1. Deberías (Debes) leer los poemas antes de venir a clase.
     2. Deberías (Debes) estudiar las fechas importantes.
     3. Deberías (Debes) saber los verbos irregulares.
     4. Deberías (Debes) ir al laboratorio más frecuentemente.
     5. Deberías (Debes) pintar una hora todos los días.

Answers

2 1. Deberías   2. Deberías
   3. No deberías   4. Deberías
   5. Deberías

3 1. prestar atención   2. tomar apuntes
   3. repasar   4. hacer preguntas
   5. preocuparse

4 1. aprueba los exámenes
   2. deja los libros en casa
   3. saca buenas notas
   4. entrega la tarea   5. presta atención

5 1. pierde   2. olvida
   3. aprende de memoria   4. apunté
   5. copiar

6 1. Michelle estudia mucho para sacar
   buenas notas.
   2. Andreas y Lew repiten el vocabulario
   para aprenderlo de memoria.
   3. Megan y yo escuchamos bien para
   tomar buenos apuntes.

7 *Answers will vary.*

8 1. b   2. a   3. e   4. d

9 1. es   2. es   3. somos   4. son
   5. son   6. es   7. eres   8. ser

10 1. Amalia es bastante creativa.
   2. Toni y Dan son bastante generosos.
   3. Ben es bastante distraído.
   4. Beto y Ana son bastante honestos.

11 1. Yo soy costarricense.
   2. José Luis y Paca son mexicanos.
   3. Tú eres chileno/a.
   4. Eleanora es cubana.
   5. Nosotros somos americanos.

12 1. estoy   2. estamos   3. estoy
   4. está   5. están   6. estoy

13 1. estoy ocupado/a
   2. estás preocupado/a
   3. estamos aburridos/as
   4. están emocionados

14 1. estoy   2. es   3. es   4. están
   5. estar   6. estar

15 *Answers will vary.*

16 1. no conozco a la nueva profesora de
   computación
   2. Gaby conoce a Mateo
   3. conocemos ese restaurante que está en
   la calle Hudson
   4. mis amigos no conocen México

17 1. es más exigente que la profesora
   Chen
   2. es menos alto que Ricardo
   3. son menos caras que las zapatillas de
   Elvira
   4. es más distraída que Paquita
   5. es más floja que Li

18 1. tomamos el metro   2. va a una cita
   3. se reúne con sus amigas
   4. mira las vitrinas   5. meriendan
   6. platicar   7. hago cola

19 1. la   2. las   3. nos   4. me
   5. lo   6. los   7. la   8. te   9. lo
   10. la

20 1. puedo ayudarte (te puedo ayudar)
   2. puedes llamarme (me puedes llamar)
   3. voy a comprarlos (los voy a comprar)
   4. las mandé   5. los llamo
   6. la tengo

21 *Answers will vary.*

Chapter 5

1 1. estirarte   2. la natación
   3. remar   4. el senderismo
   5. el montañismo   6. el ciclismo

2 1. remo   2. natación   3. senderismo
   4. ciclismo   5. escalar

3 1. durmieron   2. dormimos
   3. dormiste   4. dormí   5. dormiste
   6. dormí

4 1. bajar de peso
   2. inscribirse en un gimnasio
   3. moverse   4. salta a la cuerda
   5. practica las artes marciales
   6. se mueve

5 1. saltar   2. hace, levantamos
   3. practican   4. Se inscribe

6 1. corrió   2. escribimos   3. asististe
   4. sorprendieron   5. dieron   6. salí
   7. perdimos   8. dio   9. sacudió
   10. tendiste

7 1. Corrí tres millas.
   2. Rafael se inscribió en un gimnasio el
   jueves pasado.
   3. Asistimos a la clase de ejercicios
   aeróbicos anoche.
   4. Mikaela comió muchas verduras para
   evitar la grasa.

Answers

8 1. levantamos   2. sudó   3. practicó
    4. escalé   5. saltaron   6. caminaste

9 *Answers will vary.*

10 1. forma   2. competencia   3. dedicar
    4. salud   5. hábitos   6. grasa

11 1. Necesita usted hacer régimen
    2. Evita usted la grasa
    3. Puede usted respirar profundamente
      después de hacer ejercicios aeróbicos
    4. Se relaja usted después de hacer
      ejercicio
    5. Necesita usted reducir el estrés en su
      vida

12 1. Evita la grasa.
    2. Tomas mucha agua cada día.
    3. No trabajes todo el tiempo.
    4. Caminas un poco cada día.
    5. No comas sólo carne.
    6. Respira profundamente cuando haces
      ejercicio.
    7. Duerme ocho horas todas las noches.
    8. No bebas refrescos todo el tiempo.
    9. No corras largas distancias si no corres
      frecuentemente.

13 1. No saques   2. No practiques
    3. No llegues   4. no entregues

14 1. Ve a clases de ejercicios aeróbicos.
    2. No le pongas sal a la comida.
    3. Haz abdominales todos los días.
    4. Dile adiós a la grasa.
    5. No seas flojo en tu régimen.

15 1. pude   2. pudimos   3. pudo
    4. pudieron   5. pudiste

16 1. la nariz   2. el muslo   3. el cuello
    4. relajarse

17 1. Te duele   2. te torciste
    3. te lastimaste   4. tienes calambre

18 1. me divertí   2. se olvidó
    3. se enfermó   4. se quejaron
    5. nos cansamos

19 *Answers will vary.*

Chapter 6

1 1. se sube   2. se baja   3. semáforo
    4. turista   5. conductor   6. letrero

2 1. A las nueve y media está en la parada
    del autobús.

    2. A las diez está en el edificio.
    3. A la una está en la iglesia.
    4. A las dos está en el puente.
    5. A las cinco está en el río.

3 1. sabe   2. sé   3. Saben
    4. sabemos   5. sabe

4 1. Yo sé que San Antonio está en Texas.
    2. Alicia y yo sabemos que muchos
      turistas visitan San Antonio.
    3. Fernando sabe que muchas personas
      hablan español allí.
    4. Paco y Luisa saben dónde está el
      Álamo.
    5. Loretha sabe que hay partidos de fútbol
      en el Álamodome.

5 1. Sabe usted dónde está el restaurante
      Finni
    2. Sabe usted dónde puedo comprar unos
      vestidos bonitos
    3. Saben ustedes mucho sobre la historia
      de San Antonio
    4. Sabe usted cuando fundaron la misión
      San José

6 1. conozco   2. sabe   3. conocen
    4. conoce   5. conocen   6. sabes

7 1. Conoces el Paseo del Río
    2. Conocen ustedes a algunas profesoras
      en San Antonio
    3. Conocen ustedes la Torre de las
      Américas
    4. Saben ustedes dónde está el
      Álamodome
    5. Conoce usted la Misión San José

8 *Horizontales:* 1. pasajero
    5. de ida y vuelta   7. maletero
    Verticales: 2. andén   3. jardín
    4. recorrido   6. torre

9 1. ida, vuelta   2. estación   3. andén
    4. jardín botánico   5. torre

10 *Answers will vary.*

11 1. llegamos   2. descansaron
    3. miraron   4. fuimos   5. gustó
    6. divertimos   7. compraron
    8. fuimos   9. encantó   10. comí
    11. regresamos

12 *Answers will vary.*

13 *Answers will vary.*

14 1. el mesero   2. la propina   3. traer
    4. el postre   5. la mesera   6. pedir

Answers

15 1. pedí 2. sirvió 3. pidieron
4. sirvieron 5. sirvió 6. pedimos
7. pidió 8. servimos 9. sirvieron

16 1. traje 2. trajimos 3. trajeron
4. trajo 5. trajiste

17 1. pedí 2. pidieron 3. pidió
4. trajeron 5. pedimos 6. traje
7. sirvió

18 *Answers will vary.*

19 1. frío 2. rico 3. dulce 4. picante

20 1. Está salada la sopa
2. Está rica la ensalada
3. Está frío tu bistec
4. Está dulce el helado
5. Está picante la salsa

21 *Answers will vary.*

Chapter 7

1 1. hablaba 2. comían
3. escribíamos 4. ponías
5. dábamos 6. compraban 7. bebía
8. salías 9. vivían 10. estudiaba

2 1. tenía 2. estaba 3. vivía
4. jugábamos 5. nadaba 6. corrían
7. pasabas

3 1. El escritor Carlos Fuentes escribía
muchas cartas.
2. La cantante Linda Ronstadt cantaba
canciones para su padre.
3. El artista Pablo Picasso pintaba a la
gente de su pueblo.
4. La tenista Arantxa Sánchez Vicario
practicaba el tenis todos los días.
5. El jugador de fútbol americano Dan
Marino hacía mucho ejercicio.

4 *Answers will vary.*

5 *Answers will vary.*

6 1. iban, veían 2. iba, veía
3. íbamos, veíamos 4. iba, veía
5. iba, veía

7 *Horizontales:* 1. construir 5. pelear
6. travesuras 7. compartir
Verticales: 1. chistes 2. trepar
3. soñar con 4. asustarse

8 1. e 2. y 3. e 4. y 5. e
6. y 7. e 8. e

9 1. u 2. o 3. o 4. u 5. u
6. o 7. u 8. o 9. u 10. u

10 1. eras 2. era 3. eran 4. era
5. éramos

11 *Answers will vary.*

12 *Answers will vary.*

13 1. Claudia era solitaria.
2. Mis dos hermanos eran aventureros.
3. Mi madre era bondadosa.
4. Yo era impaciente.
5. Hernán era egoísta.
6. Tú eras conversador/a.

14 1. ruido 2. contaminación
3. gigantesco 4. ruidoso 5. sencillo

15 1. gigantescos 2. tránsito 3. ruido
4. contaminación 5. fábricas
6. sencilla

16 1. la calefacción 2. el agua corriente
3. el aire acondicionado 4. la estufa

17 1. Había menos violencia en mi ciudad.
2. Había más árboles en los parques.
3. Había menos hoteles en las playas.
4. Había menos tránsito en las ciudades.
5. Había menos contaminación del aire
también.

18 1. era 2. era 3. había 4. era
5. había 6. Había 7. era

19 *Answers will vary.*

20 1. Pablo es tan independiente como Jazz.
2. Jazz es tan fuerte como Pablo.
3. Pablo es tan bonito como Jazz.
4. Jazz es tan rebelde como Pablo.
5. Pablo es tan inteligente como Jazz.
6. Jazz es tan impaciente como Pablo.

21 1. Gilberto es tan fuerte como Rafael.
2. Alejo es tan alto como Andrés.
3. Ricardo llegó tan tarde como Paco.
4. Emilio corrió tan rápido como Sergio.
5. Gustavo es tan grande como Francisco.

22 1. tantas 2. tanta 3. tantos
4. tantos 5. tanto 6. tantos

23 1. Hay tantos plátanos como piñas.
2. Hay tantos refrescos de naranja como
refrescos de limón.
3. Hay tantas naranjas como piñas.
4. Hay tanta leche como jugo de naranja.
5. Hay tanta carne de res como pollo.

Answers

Chapter 8

1 1. inteligentísimo   2. buenísimas
3. dificilísimas   4. altísimos
5. rapidísimos   6. guapísima
7. interesantísima

2 *Answers will vary.*

3 1. a   2. c   3. a   4. b   5. c
6. a   7. b   8. b

4 1. el cocodrilo   2. el mono   3. el loro
4. la tortuga   5. la serpiente

5 1. Lupita Cárdenas es la estrella más bella de Hollywood.
2. *Galaxias VI* tiene los efectos especiales más maravillosos del festival.
3. *Silvio* fue el estreno menos popular del festival.
4. Felipe Sooner es el director más original de hoy.

6 *Answers will vary.*

7 1. la peor   2. los mejores   3. la peor
4. las mejores

8 a. 4   b. 5   c. 1   d. 6   e. 3
f. 2

9 1. Ella llevó el carro al taller.
2. Ella pasó por la farmacia.
3. Ella llevó el carro a la gasolinera.
4. Ella pasó por el banco.
5. Ella pasó por el correo.

10 1. Anoche yo soñé con ser un jugador profesional de fútbol americano.
2. Me acuerdo de que hablé con Mike Shanahan.
3. Me dijo que fue necesario aumentar de peso para jugar bien.
4. El siguiente domingo asistí a mi primer partido profesional.
5. Después del partido Troy Aikman y yo quedamos en jugar otra vez el lunes por la noche.

11 1. por   2. a   3. con   4. por
5. en

12 1. jugaba   2. hablábamos
3. levantaba   4. asistían   5. corría
6. te estirabas

13 *Answers will vary.*

14 1. desfile   2. disfraz   3. decorar
4. festival   5. carrozas
Final word: divertirse

15 1. Festival   2. desfile   3. carroza
4. decorar   5. disfraz

16 1. dijiste   2. dije   3. dijo
4. dijeron   5. dijimos   6. dijo
7. dijo   8. dijeron

17 1. Anita me dijo que la música era muy buena.
2. Miguel y Carmen me dijeron que todos estaban muy contentos.
3. Susana me dijo que estaba muy cansada después de la fiesta.
4. Tú me dijiste que la comida estaba deliciosa.
5. Y Sofía me dijo que a ella no le gustaba la música.

Chapter 9

1 1. B   2. A   3. C   4. D   5. E

2 *Answers will vary.*

3 1. Beban   2. Cierren   3. No abran
4. No escriban   5. No coman
6. Esperen

4 *Answers will vary.*

5 1. vaya   2. Siga   3. Busque
4. Vayan   5. Pidan   6. lleguen

6 1. No, no jueguen con la serpiente.
2. No, no despierten al cocodrilo.
3. No, no le den sus hamburguesas a la tortuga.
4. No, no pesquen allí.
5. No, no toquen esas plantas.

7 1. se sienten   2. se bañen
3. Lávense   4. Cepíllense
5. se afeiten   6. se pongan
7. Acuéstense

8 1. ¡Despiértese a tiempo con los despertadores Cascabel!
2. ¡No se vista si no se va a poner los bluejeans de Vaquero!
3. ¡Séquese con las toallas Suavecitas!
4. ¡No se lave el pelo con champú ordinario! ¡Use Lavabella!
5. ¡Báñese con nuestro jabón Esencia!

9 *Answers will vary.*

10 1. dependiente   2. cliente   3. etiqueta
4. escaparate   5. probadores
6. cajera   7. par   8. caja

Answers

11 1. Las botas de Claudette son menos caras
que las botas de Laura.
2. Los zapatos de Claudette son menos
caros que los zapatos de Laura.
3. La falda de Claudette es más barata que
la falda de Laura.
4. La blusa de Claudette es tan barata
como la blusa de Laura.
5. El vestido de Claudette es tan pequeño
como el vestido de Laura.
6. La falda de Claudette es más grande que
la falda de Laura.
7. Las blusas de Claudette son más
grandes que las blusas de Laura.
8. Las botas de Claudette son más grandes
que las botas de Laura.

12 *Answers will vary.*

13 1. al aire libre   2. en barata
3. descuento   4. dos por uno
5. gratis   6. ganga

14 1. te   2. me   3. los   4. las
5. las   6. nos

15 1. ¿Dónde los compra?
2. ¿Dónde la escuchan?
3. ¿Dónde las ve?
4. ¿Dónde los encuentran?

Chapter 10

1 1. aguacero   2. trueno   3. despejado
4. húmedo   5. rayo   6. nublado
7. niebla   8. tormenta

2 1. húmedo   2. niebla   3. despejado
4. trueno   5. aguacero   6. nublado
7. rayos

3 1. era   2. eran   3. era   4. éramos
5. Eran

4 1. esperaba   2. entró   3. llegó
4. Hablaba   5. pedí   6. escribía

5 1. estudiaba   2. llamó
3. hablábamos   4. llegó
5. comíamos   6. entró

6 1. Eran las ocho de la noche.
2. Carlos caminaba por el parque.
3. Esta vez Ricardo no estaba con él.
4. Hacía frío y había mucha niebla.
5. Carlos pensaba que estaba solo pero...

7 *Answers will vary.*

8 *Horizontales:* 1. despiden   4. casan
5. duermo   *Verticales:* 2. pierdo
3. van   4. cae

9 1. oyó, Creyó   2. oyó, Creyó   3. leyó
4. oyeron, se cayeron   5. oyó

10 1. hadas   2. princesa   3. ladrón
4. enano   5. madrina   6. príncipe

11 1. planetas   2. estrella   3. OVNI
4. galaxia   5. nave espacial

12 1. vivían   2. era   3. se despertó
4. se tomó   5. tuvieron   6. decidieron
7. habló   8. volvió

13 1. vivía   2. estaba   3. llovía
4. bajó   5. vio   6. pensó
7. llevaron   8. llegó   9. se cayó
10. perdió

14 1. Hace mucho tiempo vivía una tortuga
en la selva.
2. La tortuga era el animal más rápido de
la selva.
3. Un día llegó un loro.
4. El loro creía que podía correr más
rápido que la tortuga.
5. Los animales decidieron hacer una
carrera.
6. Empezó la competencia a las seis de la
mañana.
7. El loro terminó de primero y la tortuga
de segundo.
8. Al final la tortuga decidió ser el animal
más lento de la selva.

15 *Answers will vary.*

16 1. chismoso   2. noticias   3. furioso
4. romper con   5. chisme

17 1. romper   2. chisme   3. furioso
4. chismoso   5. hacer las paces
6. metiche

18 1. tuvimos   2. tuviste   3. tuve
4. tuvieron   5. tuvo

19 *Answers will vary.*

Chapter 11

1 1. el smog
2. la destrucción de las selvas tropicales
3. la contaminación del mar
4. el desperdicio del petróleo

ANSWERS

Answers

2 1. medio ambiente
2. contaminación del aire   3. smog
4. capa de ozono   5. químicos
6. solución

3 1. No debemos tirar ningún químico en la basura.
2. Nadie debe contaminar los océanos.
3. Ni el smog ni la destrucción de las selvas es bueno.
4. No debemos tirar el plástico en la basura tampoco.
5. Muchas fábricas no hacen nada para evitar la contaminación.

4 1. Nadie separa la basura.
2. No podemos nunca evitar los problemas del smog.
3. Tampoco podemos evitar la contaminación del mar.
4. Nadie puede hacer nada para mejorar la situación.
5. Nunca vamos a vivir en un lugar sin contaminación.

5 *Answers will vary.*

6 *La contaminación del aire:* el cóndor, el águila, las aves, el murciélago, los insectos *La contaminación del mar:* la ballena, los delfines, los peces

7 *Horizontales:* 3. murciélago   5. peces
6. ballena   *Verticales:* 1. delfines
2. águila   4. insecto

8 1. por   2. tanto   3. urgente
4. enfrentar

9 1. sí   2. no   3. no   4. sí
5. no   6. sí   7. sí   8. sí

10 1. acuerdo   2. siento   3. parece
4. razón   5. Así   6. contrario
7. equivocas   8. punto   9. Eso

11 *Answers will vary.*

12 1. cooperación, cooperation
2. situación, situation
3. salvar, save
4. animales, animals
5. extinción, extinction
6. eliminar, eliminate
7. destrucción, destruction
8. tropicales, tropical
9. conservar, conserve
10. energía, energy

13 1. Tiras algo de plástico en la basura
2. Conoces a alguien en una organización ecológica
3. Siempre apagas la luz cuando sales de tu cuarto
4. Sabes algo de las aves en peligro de extinción
5. Hablas con alguien sobre los problemas del medio ambiente

14 1. energía   2. apagar   3. empacados
4. mantener   5. reciclaje   6. reciclar

15 *Answers will vary.*

16 1. Podemos eliminar el smog si no usamos los carros todos los días.
2. Si evitamos los productos empacados tiramos menos basura.
3. Si reciclamos podemos mantener limpia la ciudad.
4. Si apagamos las luces conservamos más energía.
5. Si cambiamos nuestro estilo de vida mejoramos la situación.

17 *Answers will vary.*

18 1. ¡Reciclemos el aluminio, las latas y el vidrio!
2. ¡Vengamos al colegio a pie o en bicicleta!
3. ¡Mantengamos limpias las calles!
4. Al salir del baño, apaguemos las luces.
5. Seamos más responsables.

19 *Answers will vary.*

20 *Answers will vary.*

21 *Answers will vary.*

Chapter 12

1 1. Con cariño...   2. Querido/a...
3. Te echo mucho de menos.
4. Dale un saludo de mi parte.
5. Un abrazo de...

2 1. Querido   2. echo   3. menos
4. Gracias   5. dale   6. saludo
7. abrazo

3 *Answers will vary.*

4 1. monté   2. encontramos
3. se quedaron   4. albergue
5. te quedaste

5 1. Se quedó en un albergue juvenil.
2. Se quedó en casa.

114 Grammar and Vocabulary Workbook, Teacher's Edition

¡Ven conmigo! Level 2, Answers

Answers

3. Encontró un empleo.
4. Se quedó con unos parientes.
5. Montó en tabla de vela.

6 *Answers will vary.*

7 *Answers will vary.*

8 1. estaba   2. hacía   3. esquiábamos
4. llegábamos   5. teníamos   6. comía
7. pedían   8. quería   9. vivías

9 *Answers will vary.*

10 1. Ben y Carmen iban a Puerto Rico y
veían a su tío.
2. Maribel iba a Chicago y veía a su
familia.
3. Rafa y yo íbamos a Ecuador y veíamos
a muchos turistas.
4. Tú ibas a California y veías a Ignacio,
¿no?
5. Yo iba a Texas y veía los murciélagos de
Austin.

11 1. era   2. éramos   3. era   4. eran
5. eras *Final answer:* Elvis Presley

12 *Answers will vary.*

13 1. La señora Ramírez leía el periódico
cuando oyó un ruido.
2. Los niños jugaban en el jardín cuando
empezó a llover.
3. El abuelo dormía cuando el perro saltó
encima de la cama.
4. Darío hacía tarea cuando el vecino
llamó.
5. Nosotros veíamos televisión cuando
Luisito apagó las luces.
6. Sara tocaba el piano cuando entró su
hermano.
7. Yo ponía la mesa cuando se cayó un
vaso.

14 1. lavaba   2. vio   3. era   4. tenía
5. examinaba   6. abrió   7. salieron
8. querían   9. hacía

15 a. 3   b. 1   c. 5   d. 4   e. 2

16 *Horizontales:* **3.** Inmediatamente
6. pronto *Verticales:* **1.** viene
2. Para   **4.** Dentro   **5.** Algún

17 *Answers will vary.*

18 1. Vas a vivir con tus padres
2. Quiénes van a pagar tus estudios
3. Van a asistir a la universidad tú y tus
amigos

4. Qué van a estudiar
5. Qué van a ser

19 *Answers will vary.*

20 *Answers will vary.*

21 1. me gradúe   2. llegue   3. termine
4. regrese   5. asista   6. tenga